Parables
of Conversion

Lou Ruoff

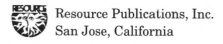
Resource Publications, Inc.
San Jose, California

Reprint Department
Resource Publications, Inc.
160 E. Virginia Street #290
San Jose, CA 95112-5876
408-286-8505 (voice)
408-287-8748 (fax)

Library of Congress Cataloging in Publication Data
Ruoff, Lou, 1946-
    Parables of conversion / Lou Ruoff.
        p.   cm.
    Includes index.
    ISBN 0-89390-403-1 (pbk.)
    1. Church year sermons. 2 Catholic Church—Sermons.
    3. Story sermons. 4. Sermons. American. 5. Ruoff, Lou, 1946- .
    I. Title.
    BX1756.R83P374 1997
    252'.02—dc21   96-40258

Printed in the United States of America

01 00 99 98 97 | 5 4 3 2 1

Editorial director: Nick Wagner
Prepress manager: Elizabeth J. Asborno
Copyeditor: Ruthann Stolzman
Production assistant: Kathi Drolet

To Vince, a friend,
who has seen me
evolve
   from a laborer
   to a preacher,
sharing and proclaiming
the Word of God.

And

To Mary and her three
children, who are seeds
of God's love for others.

To Amos, Amaziah said: "Off with you, visionary, flee to the land of Judah! There earn your bread by prophesying, but never again prophesy in Bethel; for it is the king's sanctuary and a royal temple." Amos answered Amaziah, "I was no prophet, nor have I belonged to a company of prophets; I was a shepherd and a dresser of sycamores. The LORD took me from following the flock, and said to me, Go, prophesy to my people Israel. Now hear the word of the LORD!" (Am 7:12-16).

We must constantly bear in mind that our faith started in storytelling. "In the past God spoke to our ancestors many times and in many ways through the prophets, but in these last days he has spoken to us through his Son (Heb 1:1-2 [*Good News Bible*]). And how did Jesus speak to us? He spoke in stories. He was the storyteller par excellence. His stories are from real life: stories about farming and fishing, weddings and funerals, saints and hypocrites, prodigal sons and self-righteous humbugs. He taught and he preached in pictures. "He would not speak to them without using parable" (Mk 4:34).

During the period of oral tradition his stories were told and retold and when the first gospel came to be written its most striking characteristic was its vivid storytelling. Mark was a born storyteller who filled his pages with unforgettable pictures. So the story came first and theology second. The latter really began as a reflection on story and in due course creeds, dogmas and catechisms were super-imposed on the storytelling process. There is now a notable revival in storytelling, a shift from the dogmas and creeds which dominated our thought patterns in the past, to what is now called narrative theology.

Thank God I have experienced this transition in a ministry which has passed largely from a word culture into an image culture where the Christian message must be presented visually if it is to gain access to the minds and hearts in the pews (James A. Feehan, *Story Power! Compelling Illustrations for Preaching and Teaching* [San Jose: Resource Publications, Inc., 1994], xii).

■ Contents

■ Acknowledgments

Being able to share my insights from my experiences and interweave them with the Scriptures—or vice versa—is a blessing that I never expected and cherish. I give thanks to a God who has called me by name. I give thanks to a God who has called all people into a ministry of service and love, each by name!

I thank "the people of God" of my community for all their support and love over the last four-plus years. In particular, I owe gratitude to
> Rosemary and Jim Smith (deceased),
> Bernie and José Caramat,
> Karen and Joe Coffman,
> Robin Cholewa,
> Dan Cholewa,
> Joe and Clare Reagan,
> Frank and Mary Price,
> Sandy and Dan Batkin,
> Dan and Karen Owens,

Parables of Conversion

who have supported me immensely as I have been about my travels. Most especially, I thank Mary Ann Allen, my proof-reader, whose skill makes all this possible.

■ "He took bread...and gave it to them"

3rd Sunday of Easter (A)   **Luke 24:13-35**

I grew up in the pre-Vatican II era. During this period, the Eucharist was given to us as a wafer so white, round and thin, that it immediately took root in the upper part of my mouth—and God forbid that anyone should ever touch it. The host was placed in people's mouth by the priest since it was believed that because of our sinfulness, human hands shouldn't be touching "the Body of Christ." It was instilled in every Catholic that one should pay the "proper respect" while receiving the host.

I didn't understand the logic of these rules back in those days, but as a child, it did seem reasonable. It seemed to me, however, that a God
> so great and powerful,
> so creative and loving,
> so forgiving and ever-present,

wouldn't have minded us touching "the Body of Christ," because it was God's desire to come into our sinful world as a human being and experience life as humans do every day. Obviously, Vatican II agreed, for it allowed the host to be placed on the hand, a much more realistic way of sharing the meal of Jesus. Unleavened bread, as prescribed by Church law, was also introduced at the same time. It helped me to understand the basic culture not only of my own time, but also of the time of Jesus as well; that is, bread given is bread that nourishes.

It isn't that there is any less respect for the mystery of the Eucharist, indeed for me, it enhances the reality of a caring and compassionate God coming among us despite our failings and weaknesses. In my mind, no greater example can be found "in the breaking of the bread," than when Jesus, after his crucifixion, appeared
> among his disciples,
> those very disciples
> who lost faith in the Master's very words, and
>> chose to break bread with them as the
>> risen Lord.

The meaning of Eucharist is that we fallen people are continually given the Lord's nourishment to help us be true disciples of Jesus and to be invigorated for the mission that lies ahead.

But some long-standing beliefs or habits are hard to overcome.

After being in my present parish for some six months, an elderly gentleman—and I mean a gentleman—came to me with his wife after our Sunday liturgy. He had a problem. That problem was that he wanted hosts instead of the bread that is customary of our celebration. I explained that the custom that was in place in our community, long before my arrival, was that "the people of God" make the bread themselves, and this is symbolic not only of the community being nourished by Jesus, but by their own people as well. The gentleman didn't quarrel with the rationale that I gave him, but he still wanted the host. I then explained that Jesus himself used the bread of his time, and that by using those ingredients as allowed by the Church, we are using the same type of bread as did the Lord. But again, as gently as he could, the elderly man said he didn't care what the explanation was, he simply wanted the hosts of his upbringing. I then shared with the gentleman that the hosts (wafers) were manufactured in a state far away from our own, thereby losing the personal touch that our community was proud of. Again, ever so gently, the man claimed it just didn't resonate with him. He left as politely as he had arrived, without being able to accept the reasons and logic given him.

Each Sunday, the gentleman received communion without any questions. Months went by before he approached me with the same concerns. Again, I could not help him resolve his dilemma.

After that, every several months, the gentleman would approach me with the same conversation. And as with our previous encounters, nothing was ever settled, though there was an abundance of politeness and goodwill.

Then one special Sunday, the gentleman came to church as usual, received communion, and left feeling spiritually nourished. When he returned home, his wife started cooking the breakfast that would give him the nourishment that would carry him through the day. As the gentleman sat at the kitchen table, eating his toast, he told his wife the toast was so good that he wouldn't mind having more. With that, his wife put more toast in the toaster. Suddenly she heard a voice,
> and something hitting the breakfast table.
> Death came suddenly,
> swiftly,
> immediate—and with finality.

Immediately, the gentleman left that breakfast table to
join all the Saints in the Kingdom of God at the Banquet
Table. A feast that has its own finality. We call it eternity.
I suspect the gentleman
      is very happy,
      is very much at peace,
      is very much loved, loved beyond all telling,
      and we hear that the bread in heaven is truly
         that good!

Russell Shepherd, RIP.

■ "Offer no resistance to injury" (a children's liturgical play)

7th Sunday of Ordinary Time (A)   **Matthew 5:38-48**

This act-of-violence play is based on the book *Dana Doesn't Like Guns Anymore* by Carole W. Moore-Slater (New York: Friendship Press, 1992).

Narrator: *(Begins by citing the reasons why this play is so important for all of us as we strive to be a viable Christian community. Sets the stage for the boys, Rick and Steve, and their relationship to one another and the impact television has on the young people of our nation. Cites values parents, church, and school should impart to their children.)*

Scene I: The Den

Setting: two boys, Steve and Rick, who are cousins and best friends, come in from the mall, where they had been playing games. They immediately turn on the TV/VCR in the den of Rick's house. While flipping, they stop at a scene in New York where bombs have gone off at the World Trade Center.

Rick: Wow, look at all that; that's so cool. Isn't that neat, Steve?

Steve: Yeah, it looks like that experiment you screwed up the science fair.

Rick: Shut up stupid! You couldn't do that experiment if your life depended on it. (*Shoving* Steve *out of his way,* Rick *starts flipping TV channels; he stops when he catches a local news program showing a shooting in a bar up the street.*) Hey, check that out, dude! Rifles! Sub-machine guns! I got rifles that look just like that only they don't shoot real bullets. I wish they were real. You've seen my dad's room before. He has a bunch of old rifles. He's even got some real handguns in his dresser drawer; he keeps them to protect our house.

Steve: My dad says guns are wrong and he won't let me have any. There are no guns in my house—real or toy.

Rick: Not any!? (*surprised*)

Steve: No. (*apologetically*)

Rick: No b.b. guns!? *(disbelieving)*

Steve: Nope. *(shaking his head, almost embarrassed)*

Rick: How 'bout cap guns? *(less disbelieving)*

Steve: Nope. *(a bit less embarrassed)*

Rick: Not even a squirt gun? *(now accepting the fact)*

Steve: No.

Rick: My dad says it's okay for boys to play with guns 'cause someday when they grow up and are real men, they'll need to know how to use them. *(Changes the channel once again.* Terminator II *comes on).* Look at that! Wow! Violence is all around us. Your dad doesn't live in the real world. *(Now standing in a confronting stance facing* Steve*).* You people live in some sort of dream world where everything is all love and peace. Don't you know that to get anywhere, you have to fight—even if you are protecting yourself.

Steve: *(Not giving an inch, goes face-to-face with Rick.)* You're really stupid! That's all you know: fightin' 'n killin', fightin' 'n killin'; when are you ever going to grow up?

Rick: You're a sissy like your old man. My dad says your old man is a chicken.

He's the only one who was against going to war in Iraq—a no good chicken!

Steve: (*Stares right into Rick's eyes, pausing as if he doesn't quite know what to say next.*) I'd like to punch your head in! (*filled with anger*)

Rick: Why don't you try? I dare you! (*with a half smile, though anger visible*)

Steve: My dad is good. His only mistake was having a screwball brother like your father!

Rick: Your old man is a wimp! Face it! Ha! (*very insulting*)

Steve: Take that back, you stupid jerk. Your dad's a redneck! We're ashamed to be related to scum.

Rick: Yeah, well you don't have to be. I'm gonna get my b.b. gun and take care of you right now. (*Both boys go in different directions.*)

Narrator: Both boys leave with different ideas. Rick is angry because he doesn't like anyone who sees things differently. To teach Steve a lesson, he is going to confront him with his b.b. gun. Steve, on the other hand, is scared. He knows what he said was totally unlike him. There were feelings that he kept inside. Never did he ever expect to share them with his cousin. Now facing the consequences of his words brings Steve to a position of defending himself against attack, for Steve knows Rick is true to his word. Remembering seeing guns in his uncle's dresser drawer, he feels compelled to quickly grab one of the handguns. Rick is searching in his toy chest for the b.b. gun that will scare the pants off of Steve. Meanwhile Steve searches his uncle's dresser. When both boys find what they are looking for, they come back to the den where the conversation first took place. *(Rick and Steve come face-to-face with each other with their guns. A loud shot is heard. Rick screams and falls to the floor.)*

Steve: *(Realizing what has transpired, he screams as he runs toward Rick, dropping his gun.)* Rickie, Rickie, I'm sorry! Oh, God, help me! I lost my head! I'm sorry!

Scene II: The Hospital

Narrator: In our society, a young boy being shot is not all that uncommon. Our scene now takes us to General Hospital, where Rick's family has been waiting to hear about his condition after an emergency operation. The doctor will be informing Rick's parents.

Doctor: Are you Rick's parents?

Rick's Dad:	We are. How is he?
Doctor:	He'll be okay. I'm sure the police have already spoken to you?
Rick's Dad:	Yes, they have. Can we see our son?
Doctor:	I'll take you to him. I want you to hear what I have to say to him. (*They enter Rick's room.*) Rick, I'm the doctor who operated on you. I wanted your parents to hear what I'm telling you. You're very lucky. The Lord must have been with you. That bullet just grazed your side. It could have been your heart. You lost a lot of blood, and I'm sure you're sore—but you're going to be fine. Remember this, and you have a scar to prove it: guns can hurt—even kill.

Scene III: The Den

Narrator:	It has been some time since the shooting incident. Rick and Steve's parents have had time to reflect and assess where they are as family and responsible citizens. Rick and Steve are present for this "family discussion."
Rick's Dad:	I really don't know what to say. I'm still very angry at this whole incident. My son almost lost his life at the hands of my brother's son; yet, we call ourselves family. (*Pause*) But I'm glad we've gathered to discuss our

	feelings—and see if we can pick up the pieces. I think Steve wants to say something.
Steve:	I've been staying inside since all this happened. I feel so stupid. I haven't been at school 'cause I feel embarrassed and don't want to meet or talk to anyone about this. So I'm glad we got together. I want to say that I'm sorry for all that's happened. All I know, when Rick and I were fighting, all I felt was hatred. (*Pause*) I guess I could have done something else; I was just stupid.
Steve's Dad:	Son, there was a lot you could have done. You allowed your anger to get the best of you. You could have walked away. Isn't that what I've taught you?
Steve:	Rick, I'm sorry. I hope we can still be friends.
Rick:	I've been mad ever since that day. I've never been in the hospital before—and that's scary. I still feel sore but still mad 'cause it could have been worse. I still want to be friends but I think to myself what happens if we get into another argument. I still have to think about it all.
Rick's Dad:	I think the responsibility is on all of us—myself, most especially. When I heard of the shooting I felt like tearing Steve to pieces—and his

father with him. I had to think this out myself. I've lived my life thinking I'm a sort of Rambo, protecting all of us. But in fact, I'm just as much to blame for this act of violence because that's how I always settled everything in life. I think I need to rethink my priorities—and see if guns are that important to have in my home.

Steve: *(Moving toward Rick)* Maybe we can try to be friends again, like beginning from scratch again. *(offering his hand)*

Rick: I'll try. *(shaking hands)*

■ Total Trust in God

Feast of the Assumption   **Luke 1:39-56**

We live in
        an age of doubt,
        an age of skepticism,
        an age of outright disbelief.
It goes from
        Presidents,
        Popes,
        the Congress
        the press,
        from pastors to everyone in the pews.
Few, if any, are believed. Many of us are called into
question about as often as we
        put on, take off our shoes.
Yet, each of us uses the word "trust" as often as we
        put on, take off our clothes.
I have observed every presidential campaign since 1960,
and I don't remember a single campaign that didn't use
and over-use that "trust" word. We cannot
        make a deal,
        buy food,
        pay our rent,

>   purchase land,
>   cash our checks
>   without using currencies inscribed with the
>   words "In God We Trust."

But trust in God—even in God—is not an easy proposition, given the everyday experiences of life. Mary, the mother of Jesus, is truly the exception. The trust Mary had in God was so total that we remember her uniquely throughout the Church year. It is Mary's words as seen in Luke's Gospel that serve to make us people eager to put our trust in God, and be followers of her Son. Because Mary trusted in God so totally, she bore God's Son and became his first disciple. In that way, Mary honored her God.

Few of us are like Mary. Few of us know total trust. Though this past week, I've seen several of my parishioners dying in the hospital—and I'm awed at their trust in God in the midst of sickness and illness and death. I can only marvel at their faith—and the faith of their families and loved ones. It challenges me in a loving way to be more trusting in God in my own hectic life. And that's the value that Mary has to offer us. In truth, we are more like the disciple Peter in regard to our faith and trust. If you remember, Peter, one of the more obnoxious of Jesus' companions, told everyone of his faith and how he trusted in the Lord unequivocally. I'm sure his friends said "sure" in some affectionate way. For they knew that as soon as Peter was in any way caught in the raging waters of life, his faith would sink like a bathtub in the ocean. Most, if not all of us, are like Peter. We sink in the face

>   of despair,
>   of envy,
>   of pride
>   of greed
>   of anger,
>   of hate

and as we sink, we begin the process of hurting one another and ourselves. And we sink even deeper *until* we call upon Jesus to rescue us—as with Peter.

Mary's trust was total.

Luke's Gospel gives us two portraits of Mary. The first is the young woman who is troubled upon hearing the words of the angel Gabriel of a message from God. After Gabriel reassures her, he tells her she is to bear the Son of God. Mary answers "May it be…"

After Vatican II some Catholics thought that Mary had been pushed out of the doors in many churches. But those with sincere hearts know that Mary is central to our understanding of an active God in our lives.

The words of the Magnificat are inspiring to me each morning of my life. During the time I've taken my ministry to heart, I have relied on those words for my "trusting the Lord" everyday. But in heart, the praise Mary gives to God is the prayer of each of us to the Lord who has raised us from our lowliness and given us every good thing. Thus each of us can give birth to the spirit of Jesus to our neighbors—near and far.

Trusting in God everyday is not easy. It takes a special understanding to see just where God is involved in our lives—and act upon it.

In my early twenties, I was stabbed and critically hurt. Even in those moments that death was near, I had enormous anger for the one who did this to me. During many months in the hospital I plotted to do harm; my desire for vengeance was frightening. I was resolved to settle accounts the day I could walk away from the hospital. My intention was to do severe damage to the one who hurt me.

Over that period of time, however, I met someone who loved me and, in many ways, committed his life to me. I couldn't quite figure it out at the time that this love given me was in fact love reborn in me that could later be shared. Instead of continuing to plot and connive ways of getting even, I found myself caught in the mystery of this person who cared about me and wondered *"Why?"* Why would this person take so much
> time,
>
> money,
>
> energy,
>
> patience
>> from his life to give to me.

Years later he himself gave me the answer. He told me that he had trusted in God enough that there would be a purpose for me in all my lowliness.

That's why the Magnificat of Mary is close to me. Each of us needs to put his trust in someone. Someone special put his trust in me. That trust allowed me to be accepted and presented me a purpose in life. By this acceptance and trust, I was finally able to trust and accept others.

In our need to trust someone, we can look at Luke's portrait of Mary. We have the same God as Mary and as she gave her total trust to her God, each of us needs to put the same total trust in our God as well. Each of us began from nowhere—yet are called to service and discipleship in the mission of Jesus. Jesus is there to help us transform ourselves and reassure us that there is a purpose for us.

By the way, the one who hurt me is now my best friend!

We're called to be *transformation* people: from hate to *love.*

John Wozniak, MD, passed away March 1993.

■ Jesus Walks the Water of the Sea

19th Sunday of Ordinary Time (A)   **Matthew 14:22-33**

Jesus promised his disciples they could move mountains if they continued to have faith. "Faith," said Jesus, "would have you

>move mountains
>move skyscrapers,
>move the cause of history by
>moving people;
>moving people to change,
>moving people to accept my law,
>moving people to love Me,
>moving people to love God,
>moving people to love one another."

Then one day while the disciples were about their business, fishing at sea, they caught a glimpse of Jesus standing—indeed walking on the water of the sea! Peter seeing this spectacle, and impetuous as always, immediately jumped out of the boat, and also began

walking on the water, moving toward Jesus. Peter might
have done better if he had
> water skied,
> water glided,
or even waited for the weather to have gotten cold enough
and ice skated toward Jesus. But Peter chose to walk.

In retrospect, Peter would have had better success
walking in space—or even walking on the moon. But walk
Peter did—until he thought about what Jesus had said,
"With faith, you will be able to move mountains..." And
now, with every step, Peter began slipping into the water,
becoming aware his faith was faltering; each nervous
stride brought Peter to the brink of drowning in the abyss
of the sea.

Then,
> grappling with the forces of the sea;
> gasping for breath, for air, for time,
> > for life itself; and
> grabbing to hold on to Jesus,
Peter realizing his fate depended on the Master who was
before him—and the Master's faith.

The strength of Jesus' arm was enough to pull the
nearly-drowned, pot-bellied Peter to his bosom, holding
the disciple tightly and securely until they reached the
boat.

As Peter was composing himself, lying with fish and net
on the floor of the boat, with water oozing from his
garments, and the disciples puzzled as to his intent, Peter
felt terribly embarrassed. Jesus, knowing this
embarrassment, reassured Peter of his trust and love.

I believe Jesus, in his reassurance to Peter, must have praised his friend for his display of love, a risk that could have had Peter exuding his last breath.

Saying (or showing) "I love you" always runs the risk of rejection. What I believe Jesus is saying to those who take risks is that if rejection comes, for whatever reason, "I will be there for you."

I remember my first "I love you" and hearing the rejection. It was as if my heart burst; my faith was caught in the swirl of the rising tide—and like Peter, I began
>   to waver,
>   to falter;
I began to sink into the sea of dismay.

It took a long time to get over that single rejection. In that time, the presence of Jesus' love was evident as I grew
>   in maturity and knowledge,
>   in service and love.

Ten years later, it was my second "I love you" that brought again the rising tide, making my way rough to survive. And again, I began losing faith. Of course, Jesus' arm was there for me. But one day I asked the Master why he had a habit of rescuing people at the last possible moment. Jesus reminded me that the friend I sought advice from to pull me through this latest whirlwind was my first "I love you."

Jesus proceeded to tell me that over the years my eyes were blind to the many people who, in a thousand ways, have expressed "I love you." Jesus continued to tell me: "People have gained new perspectives about their lives because of the countless ways you have said, 'I love you.'"

In daily life Jesus is well aware that
> our intentions,
> our actions,
> our words
will signal "I love you" to many people.

The "I love you" can legitimately frighten many people;
some, however, especially those who find it hard to know
themselves, become so scared they overreact, building
walls of protection. The consequence of taking the risk of
loving is that we are liable to be jostled about, lose balance
and be swallowed up by the currents of
> frustration,
> disappointment, and
> despair.
And like Peter, Jesus will rescue and revive us—and in
due time, if we continue to hold strong our faith in the
Master, that "I love you" will become understandable.

■ "Poor Widow Contributes"

32nd Sunday of Ordinary Time (B)   **Mark 12:38-44**

In Jesus' day, the Scribes were the learned class among the Jews; they were the official authorities on the written law and oral tradition. There was a problem, however, with Scribes who demanded and received adulation and respect but seldom, if ever, respected anyone else—even widows who were poor and insecure. There are such "Scribes" in our day, and they act much the same.

On the other hand, many religious leaders are true to their commitment to the down-and-out and in return receive public adulation when such service is given authentically. Listen to a true story:

There was once a well-known Cardinal, a prince of the church, who called for reforms in a church
>   so old,
>   so spotty,
>   so wrinkled
that the winds of change failed to muster even a whimper of a breeze. Though he angered many, few could deny his virtue.

This Cardinal called for a reconciliating church rather
than an authoritarian institution stuck in age-old
problems that didn't make much sense anymore. Though
he angered many, few could deny his virtue.

This Cardinal was a leader for rights and right causes. He
championed the cause of justice:
>justice for the poor,
>justice for laborers,
>justice for the divorced,
>justice for
>>the widows,
>>the orphans,
>>the lonely.

Though he angered many, few could deny his virtue.

The Cardinal challenged
>his own hierarchy and
>his own government
>>when war was taking the lives of many.
>He called for peace.
>He called for negotiations.
>He called for reason and sanity.
>He called for patience—

the same patience God has shown people for so long.
Though he angered many, few could deny his virtue.

This Cardinal would probably have said his greatest
achievement was in the field of Civil Rights. During the
momentous struggle for black recognition and respect of
the 1960s, the Cardinal urged a complete reconstruction
of social priorities to give the black people
>a just share in the "American Dream":
>a rightful share in the housing market,
>a rightful share in the educational market,
>a rightful share in the job market,
>rightful treatment in the health care market.

Though he angered many, few could deny his virtue.

His greatest contribution, many felt, came after he retired
from active ministry in the early 1970s. Many street
people would line up regularly outside his residence and
without fail he would
> feed them,
> talk with them,
> give them hope.

Though he angered many, few could deny his virtue.

One day the Cardinal died. He was laid out in a big
cathedral—and for twenty-four hours people passed his
coffin including:
> two U.S. senators,
> a governor,
> a mayor,
> all kinds of politicians and prelates—

even a telegram from the president of the United States
was read.
> They touched.
> They mourned.
> They cried for a friend.

There *was* one man, however—almost at the very end of
the line—who came to pay his respects to the Cardinal;
> his clothes were filthy,
> he smelled offensive, and
> a wine bottle could be seen bulging from his
> back pocket.

For a moment the ushers almost stopped him from
entering the edifice.

Once inside, the man came to the coffin.
> He touched.
> He mourned.
> He cried for a friend.

Before leaving the coffin, this man opened the Cardinal's hand and slipped him a couple of dollars for his journey to heaven.

Though he angered many, few could deny his virtue.

■ Prodigal Son Parable

4th Sunday of Lent (C)   **Luke 15:11-32**

A fortunate thing happened to everyone (here) while on
the road to Easter.

Mindful of our need for reconciliation, we all have been
reconciled (tonight) by our faith.

I personally do not know
        a better story,
        a better parable
in all Scripture that deals more clearly with the
nitty-gritty of
        human circumstances,
        human feelings,
        human failures,
        human struggles, and
        human faithfulness
than the parable of the Prodigal Son. Jesus is a master
storyteller when confronting the
        presumptions,
        emotions, and
        styles

we all seem to have in common.

Now, there was a fellow of eighteen who was tempted and
seized by the "all you can get syndrome" by doing
>everything and
>anything
that seemed feasible. Money was his sole goal. This fellow
left home and traveled to a far away city. For five years
this person spent his parents' hard earned money on all
sorts of gambling:
>poker,
>blackjack,
>darts,
>pool,
>horses,
>stocks,
>football,
>baseball,
>slot machines,
>dogs,
>whatever.

The fellow
>connived,
>cheated,
>embezzled,
>lied,
and stacked the deck against almost everyone. He ruined
his good name and the reputation of his family and
friends.

Then one day this fellow faced certain bodily
disfigurement and possible death because he held out
against the "Mob." They searched the entire city for him.
This fellow was desperate and went into hiding for several
months. Finally he unlocked the imaginary handcuffs

holding his pride in check and headed for home. He
approached his mother's home.

It so happened that this person's older sister was visiting
their mother. As the young man was within sight of the
house, the mother caught sight of her exhausted son.
While he was still a block and a half away, the mother
jumped from her seat! She ran to meet him. They
> touched,
> hugged,
> kissed,
> cried,
> smiled—

and they rejoiced. She brought her son home and they
celebrated his return. There was
> laughter,
> singing,
> and dancing.

The young man's sister, however, saw all this and refused
to join the festivities, feeling resentment—for she never
had even a birthday party all the years she was growing
up. All this was for someone who never took life as
seriously as she had her entire life. So while the mother
was hugging her son, the sister
> did not,
> could not.

The sister
> allowed her feelings to handcuff her hands
> and
> allowed feelings to handcuff her heart.

She became a prisoner of her own feelings.

There was another lad of eighteen who killed two people
in a violent and greedy act involving drugs and money.
The lad in this particular story was sent to the state
penitentiary for no less than forty-eight years without
parole. The lad had lost everything:

> friends,
> family,
> freedom,
> rights, and most especially,
> dignity.

While in prison one day the lad asked the chaplain of the penitentiary to go to a distant city in search of his father who had disowned him, and whom he hadn't seen in many years. (The lad's mother had died while he was incarcerated.) A few months later the chaplain began the laborious road to reconciliation with the lad's father. The father seemed ready and even anxious, but this man's new wife allowed past failures to handcuff her heart and resisted any move to reconciliation. She insisted, "your wife or your son?"

After several meetings with the chaplain, the father who faced the possibility of losing his spouse and the fear of loneliness rejected all attempts at reconciliation. Do you suppose each of them couldn't find the key to his particular handcuff?

There was yet another man who one year ago came to (this particular) church seeking reconciliation after oh so many years of being a criminal. The man spent twenty-five years away from God and church—until last year, when he reconciled himself to the Master. The man left church fully inspired and renewed in spirit. The former met an elder son—no, he met a lot of elder sons and daughters who convinced him that his sins were really not forgiven. They told him that he wasn't suitable for the Kingdom. These elders insisted that the man put out his hands and they handcuffed them so that they would not be alone. This must never happen again, cannot happen again, because Jesus is *the key* to God's forgiveness—and *the Christ* is among us tonight.

Let us all
            rejoice in forgiveness,
            rejoice in reconciliation, and
            vow to loosen our own handcuffs—
and those of our neighbors because (tonight) we met *the
key* to our own freedom that allows us to forgive and to
accept forgiveness.

■ Sheepgate—a reflection

4th Sunday of Easter (A)   **John 10:1-10**

> ...if [people] are convinced that the one before them
> is really God-become-man, they will be able to observe
> something absolutely unique in the history of the
> world: God...coping with life on the very terms that
> [God] has imposed upon [humans]. They will be
> seeing God not seated high on a throne, but down in
> the battlefield of life (J. P. Phillips, *Your God Is Too
> Small* [New York: Macmillan Publishing Co., Inc.,
> 1977], 74. Used with permission.)

This reading from J. P. Phillips has as much to do with
the Easter experience as any reading that comes to mind.
The reading is about experiencing earthly life in order to
share in the eternal life promised to us all.

The Easter experience is
> the victory of good over evil,
> the triumph of life over death,
> the celebration of Jesus over all obstacles.

This person Jesus
> lived like us,
> worked and played like us.

The man Jesus
> worshiped like us,
> endured burden and pain like us and
> cherished memories like us.

This same Jesus accepted a unique mission from his Father to come share in our life so that we might be led to his all-personal God.

During Jesus' public ministry, he called for the reformation and rededication of people's lives to God and to one another. In this way, the Master taught, love will not only exist but mature and prosper.

Yet despite all his teaching and splendid ministry, Jesus was vilified and strung on a cross (the most humiliating kind of death in those days); his journey in our land was cut short.

Jesus' life was light; his life was life for those he touched and for those who dared to believe.

When I think about the promise of new life, I often remember a classic movie I saw as a youth. The movie, *Angels with Dirty Faces*, starred James Cagney and Pat O'Brien.

As the movie begins, two teenagers are running from the police after trying to rob a freight car in the Lower East Side of New York. One of the youths is captured while the swifter one escapes the strong arm of the law. The captured youth is Rocky Sullivan played by Cagney; the more fortunate youth is Jerry Connally played by O'Brien.

As the movie progresses Rocky is sent to reform school only to become a gangster later in life. Jerry, on the other hand, completes high school and later becomes a priest.

Twenty years pass and Rocky, at the pinnacle of his profession, comes back to his boyhood neighborhood where he meets his old friend, the-now Fr. Connally. Fr. Connally has been assigned to a run-down parish where the streets are loaded with youths with nothing to do.

Rocky, a thief and marauder in shepherd's clothing, attracts the attention and imagination of young toughs eager to follow someone. Rocky leads them into the world of dishonesty, greed, and selfishness. Moreover, Rocky shows the youths a life of crime defying human respect and dignity.

As the movie comes to a conclusion, Rocky is sentenced to die in the electric chair for his life of crime.

On the morning before his execution, Rocky is visited in prison by Fr. Connally. His old friend asks the condemned killer for one last request: "to die yellow;" that is, to die acting as if he is a coward so that the youths will see the contradiction and turn away from the road they are embarking upon. After protesting loudly, Rocky did in fact die acting like a coward. As the electric current went rushing through his body, Rocky screamed and yelled till he succumbed.

The next morning's newspaper had blaring headlines announcing the coward's death. The neighborhood toughs, forsaking their allegiance to Rocky, approached Fr. Connally as the new source of credibility.

Movies, as we know, are always nicely put together,
giving people only a hint of life; never fully able to give the
total dimension of life's reality.

In this particular movie there are, however, major
similarities that attract Christian attention.

For instance, Rocky as a thief and marauder led people to
a false understanding of life, robbing them of values, a
theme Jesus continually warned against. In the end,
Rocky, uncharacteristically, put aside the costume of
deception and allowed his death to be a source of promise
for the youngsters he sought to influence.

Jesus is the ultimate shepherd, whose humiliating death
opens the gate for the lost and bumbling sheep to bask in
his abundant love, now and forever.

■ Jesus feeds the hungry

17th Sunday of Ordinary Time (B)   **John 6:1-15**

(AP) - A 300-year drought drove people out of Northern cities in Mesopotamia, the "cradle of civilization" in what is now Iraq and Syria, and might have led to the downfall 4,000 years ago of the first great empire in history, researchers say (*The Virginian Pilot and Ledger-Star* [8/21/93]).

The rains have been plentiful....Still, in southern Sudan the old, the young and the weak are dying of starvation....As earlier in Ethiopia and Somalia, this famine is in part the result of civil war. No one knows how many are starving, but in a cycle of hatred and revenge, peace is not in sight, nor is an end to hunger (*Time Magazine* [8/23/93]).

The U.S. Government is the world's leader in exporting armaments throughout the world despite the fall of Soviet Communism. The likelihood of this to change is very doubtful (CNN, *International Hour* [8/20/93]).

In our land at a table filled aplenty with southern fried chicken, mashed potatoes, peas, broccoli, and a cucumber salad with iced tea—and, oh, that carrot cake for dessert somewhere in the kitchen—the prayer begins, "Our Father who is in heaven and holy is your name, give us this day our daily bread..."

In a far distant land at a table empty of food a cry is intoned,
"Our Father who is in heaven and holy is your name, give us
water so that we can have our daily bread..."

Water is desperately
>prayed for in Africa,
>hoped for in Africa, and
>needed in Africa.

In our land, water has always been plentiful and plentiful
water has many purposes:
>we wash "Girl", our pet German shepherd,
>we wash our 300ZX Turbo—our pride and joy,
>we wash the sand off from the beach while on
>>vacation; why,
>we even fill our pools and water beds with
>>our daily supply of water.

And if we listen, a half a world away: "Our Father who is
in heaven and holy is your name, give us *water* so that we
can have our daily bread..."

In our land the government pays very good
>bucks,
>loot,
>cash,
>money

to farmers to
>dump,
>burn, and
>destroy

surplus
>wheat,
>corn,
>oats,
>potatoes, and
>soybeans.

In this way, these commodities will maintain their market value and everybody will be happy. And if we listen, once again a half a world away: "Our Father who is in heaven and holy is your name, give us *water* so that we can have our daily *food*..."

In the Good Book, I've read some exciting stories. There was Abraham, who bargained with Yahweh to save
fifty,
forty,
thirty,
twenty,
ten, and even
five good people
and God was more than willing.

There was also Moses who had about enough while on the road to the Promised Land. The people were very hungry, some even starving, and old man Moses let God have it—and manna fell from the heavens!

And then, of course, there was Jesus who fared as well. Jesus told thousands they would have their fill when they too were hungry while on the road hearing him preach. Many of these temperamental people didn't believe Jesus and behaved somewhat foolishly and waited like children for some sort of magic to happen—but instead of magic they received a miracle. Jesus prayed, "Our Father who is in heaven and holy is your name, give us this day our daily bread," and the fish and bread kept being passed around till everyone had his fill and left.

Now, one would think after all these thousands of years people would learn from
Abraham,
Moses, and
Jesus—

and solve the dilemma in Africa.

There's a tropical storm coming up the coast:
>
> Miami was drenched,
> Jacksonville was submerged,
> Charleston was soaked, and
> Norfolk was flooded.

California, Seattle, and the entire west coast was hit
rather severely by mud slides caused by record rains.

Enormous rains are reported
>
> in London,
> in Bangkok,
> in Ireland, and
> in China.

We know God is a Master Creator. The Almighty
>
> created the skies,
> created the clouds that accompany the skies,
> and
> created the rain that gives purpose to the
> clouds, and
> created soil for the nourishment of the food
> for the earth.

But no one said God was a master navigator; the creator's
rain misses many countries that are in need of water.

We, who are richly blessed with an abundance of water,
must take on the responsibilities of being the navigators.

We must help stop the flow of armaments and sow
harmony and help start the flow of water. Then the words
"Our Father who is in heaven and holy is your name, we
thank you for our daily bread..." will be truly universal.

■ "I am the bread of life"

18th Sunday of Ordinary Time (B)   John 6:24-35

Yesterday Jesus fed the thousands with an abundance of fish and bread.

Today Jesus is saying, "I am the bread of life; whoever eats my bread will never die."

Jesus' bread is food for thought.

His bread is food for life.

His bread is indeed life. His bread *is* life.

And this promise of life is eternal, forever, timeless, continuous, and without end.

Jesus' bread is really his teaching. If we eat and digest his teaching, we will inherit that everlasting life. But sometimes his teaching is a hard meal to swallow.

Jesus' contemporaries had trouble following him. Often they could not understand his message. How could they follow someone who didn't make sense to them?

Yesterday Jesus made a lot of sense to the people.

Today Jesus is not making sense to them.

Yesterday Jesus fed them real food and everyone was pleased. They began to believe in him; there was instant credibility.

Today Jesus is talking about bread that is going to make people live forever; and he's talking about his own body. How could they not begin to call him a fraud, a fool?

Yesterday Jesus seemed rational to them. He seemed to be in command of the situation and of himself, they thought. And they were delighted.

Today Jesus is calling himself the real Bread of Life and they begin calling him
> a screwball,
> a nut,
> a lamebrain, and
> an idiot.

Yesterday Jesus gave the people real food—and they were exuberant.

Today Jesus is again offering people real food—and they are refusing. Oh, how quickly they have forgotten.

Yesterday Jesus gave the people
> his time,
> his words of hope,
> his compassion, and
> his food.

39

And they accepted gladly. The people wanted to call him
> a very clever person,
> a miracle worker,
> a prophet, and
> a king—
> and Jesus refused.

Today Jesus gives the people a way to live in happiness; a way to live in peace, a way to see goodness in all of God's creation; and a way to understand truth if only they could accept the good of himself.

The people shouted to him:
> You gave us food yesterday—and we were
> filled,
> you give us strange ideas today—and we're
> hungry again.
> You gave us hope for the future yesterday—
> you give us only thoughts today.
> You gave us reasons for believing in God
> yesterday—you give us only baloney today.
> You gave us food yesterday when we were
> hungry—why can't you give us real food
> today?
> You gave us bread yesterday and we listened
> to you,
> you gave us bread yesterday and we believed
> in you,
> you gave us bread yesterday and we offered
> to make you king.

> Give us real food today
> and we'll tolerate you,
> give us real food today
> and we'll endure one another,
> give us real food today
> and we'll put up with God.

Jesus said:

> I gave you real food yesterday,
> I will give you real food today,
> I give you real life forever,
> *You* have a choice.

■ "I am the bread that came down from heaven"

19th Sunday of Ordinary Time (B)   **John 6:41-51**

Confrontation persisted in being the activity of the day as Jesus continued speaking to the thousands he had fed the day before. It so happened that Jesus and his entourage proceeded from the mountain to a busy market place on his way to Central Park. Jesus stopped and said:

"I am the bread of life,
I am the bread from heaven.
Believe in me and you shall all live forever."

Then someone in the multitude interrupted Jesus, "You cannot be from the God of our ancestors. That God gave our ancestors manna from heaven—and it was eatable bread.

"You're only an impostor!
You're only a carpenter's son.
What do you know about life?"

Another person in the mass of people stepped forward
and spoke:
> "You're ridiculous, man!
> You're pretending to be Somebody; why,
> you're not even a college graduate, are you?"

Others chimed in: "He must be some sort of spy; a special
agent for the FBI, maybe the CIA, or worse yet the IRS!
Perhaps worse yet he's working for an Islamic terrorist
group."

Jesus looked at the meats, the poultry, and the produce that
the market was selling and retorted, "You have bodily food
here from God that your eyes recognize. You also have
spiritual food standing before your very eyes but you fail to
see him. Discard your disbelief, your suspicions, and your
pride and you will be able to see and understand."

As Jesus was leaving the marketplace to continue his
journey to Central Park, he was mobbed by a sea of
humanity outside St. Patrick's Cathedral. The throng
again began to question Jesus,
> "You give us all this malarkey about bread
> from heaven—who are you?
> You give us all this mumbo jumbo about
> living forever—who are you?
> Are you some sort of subversive?
> a libertarian?
> a communist?
> an environmentalist?
> a liberal?
> a capitalist?—who are you?"

And answering the crowd, Jesus spoke:
> "In a word, I am the Word.
> I am the bread of life and I am true
> to my word.
> In truth, I am God's Son."

Many in the crowd erupted in anger; one bitter person in
the crowd roared at Jesus,
>"Do you know where you are?
>How dare you say that in front of God's house?"

Jesus replied:
>"God's house is in people's hearts;
>God lives in hearts—not in places.

Cathedrals, churches, synagogues, mosques serve only to
nourish those hearts. I was sent to live in your hearts—if
you want me to and believe in me."

Jesus' travels took him past the New York and the
American stock exchanges with his ever-increasing
entourage. As Jesus was crossing Broad and Wall Streets,
a certain gentleman approached him saying, "This is our
life, our pulse, our bread and butter—not your bread, Sir."

Jesus responded, "You take a risk with
>your stocks and bonds,
>your commodities,
>your mutual funds, and
>your securities.

The risk you take is not foolproof; you stand the chance of
losing. But with my flesh that I give you, the risk you take
will be for the sake of life—life that knows no end."

Jesus finally made his way to Central Park and the mob
had grown three times its earlier size. Some observers
who had just arrived at the scene questioned each other
as to what was taking place:
>a political speech?
>a rock concert?
>a student rally?
>a union march?
>a Fourth of July celebration?

A businessman said he heard a rumor that some fellow was giving bread away that would guarantee life forever—and that it was all free!

The person standing beside him murmured: "No one gives anything away for free these days. It sounds like nonsense to me."

It so happened that Jesus overheard this conversation as he was walking by, sensed the speakers' emptiness of heart yet felt compassion for them. For Jesus knew they were rejecting what they knew not.

■ "My flesh is for the life of the world"

20th Sunday of Ordinary Time (B)   **John 6:51-58**

The crowd Jesus was addressing started chanting the slogan, "We need Forever bread." They wanted the "Forever bread" that guaranteed forever life. Jesus offered the people bread that would give all who ate of it everlasting life—and no questions asked.

The sea of people, becoming more curious and less belligerent than before, asked of Jesus,
> "We *need* nourishment here and now—
>   can you give us that?"
> "We *need* ample food here and now—
>   can you give us that?"
> "We *need* peaceful lives here and now—
>   can you give us that?"

Jesus answered: "I cannot give you what you *need* without a cost." The masses interrupted Jesus saying, "Yesterday you told us it was free—now you're changing your mind?"

Others in the crowd chanted, "How much, how much, how much?" Jesus replied,
> "The cost to you is nothing:
> it is free,
> no charge involved—I will pay the cost."

The crowd again spoke loudly, "We'll help you pay for this Forever bread. Where is it?
> We have credit;
> the bank managers know us.
> We have a handful of charge cards
> with no limit.
> We'll sell
> our IRAs,
> our real estate.
> We'll sell our stocks and bonds.
> Here's our cash; do you take
> personal checks?
> travelers cheques?
> cashier notes?
> foreign currency?
> We have all the IDs you'll want."

Jesus responded to all the voices, "I must bear the cost myself. What my Father will give you *must* be done through me."

The crowd, somewhat taken back, pleaded with Jesus, "If this Forever bread is to give us forever life—let us pay for it. Why should you give us Forever food and bear the cost yourself? Let us do our part."

Jesus responded:
> "Your part is simple enough to practice;
> follow my example to all people, to the
> outcast...

> Your part is simple enough to master; follow
> my example to the oppressed as you would
> the leaders...
> Your part is simply to believe in me—and to
> do the will of my Father."

But the crowd nonetheless again raised their voices to
Jesus:

> "Where's the Forever bread?"
> "How long must we wait?"
> "Are you the only one who can give us this
> Forever bread?"

Jesus simply smiled and nodded his head and said, "I
must give up my flesh to show you the love my Father and
I have for all of you; all of you

> in every age and culture,
> in every society,
> in every
>> nation,
>> city,
>> town,
>> village,
>> neighborhood,
>> street, and
>> house—

my gesture will leave no one unloved."

The crowd, finally piecing everything together; realizing
what Jesus had been telling them for days, said, "Must
you die, sir, so that we can have that Forever bread?"
Jesus said firmly, "I must." Now the crowd believing in
disbelief responded,

> "That's a crime, sir."
> "That's a shame, sir."
> "That's a pity, sir."
> "That's a sin, sir."

"No, it is not a sin," responded Jesus. "Rather, it is for your sins that I want you to have my Forever bread. I am willing to die so that you may enjoy the bread of Forever life."

With that the crowd intoned,
>   "We liked matching wits with you, sir."
>   "We liked having you around, sir."
>   "We'll surely grieve without you, sir."

And Jesus concluded, "You will eat my Forever bread and you will
>   really,
>   truly,
>   wholeheartedly
>   praise my memory,
>   rejoice in my presence, and
>   celebrate Forever!"

■ "A savior has been born"

Children's Christmas Mass   **Luke 2:1-14**

At the dawn of creation, God carved a splendid cave into a rugged and beautiful mountain. The cave stood proud in its radiance...sparkling white and shimmering in the dark of the night.

For a billion years or more the cave was left undisturbed except for animals that found shelter from the hungry predators looking for an easy kill.

Then one day the Lord God Almighty said to the cave: "Today, Cave, your mission will be to shelter and care for my people. Protect them from inclement weather, especially from the harsh winds of winter. I also want you to give refuge to people frightened by the wild beasts I have created. But your most important mission is to save my people from one another."

Then the Lord God Almighty told the cave that someday it would have a supreme mission to carry out. The excited cave begged the Lord God Almighty to explain, but the Lord did not elaborate.

Not long after the Lord spoke, a young man and woman sought sanctuary in the cave to hide from the Lord. The cave welcomed the two with great enthusiasm and hospitality. But soon the cave learned that the pair had disobeyed the Lord God. The cave was very disappointed in the behavior of the man and woman. Suddenly the voice of the Lord God Almighty was heard all over the land. The Lord wanted the couple to come out of hiding and when they refused, it was the cave who suggested they not put the Lord God to the test. The pair listened to the cave and despite their fear, they left the cave and approached the Lord.

Many years later, a young man who had just murdered his only brother fled from his house to seek haven in the cave on the outskirts of town. Once inside the cave, the man smeared his bloodied hands on the wall of the cave. This shocked and angered the cave and it hesitated to be friendly and inviting as it had been in the past. When the voice of the Lord God spoke, the cave was relieved of the harrowing experience of harboring an undesirable in its bosom.

It wasn't too many years afterward that people started using the cave as a place to plot terror against others. These unfriendly people met in the safety of the darkness the cave provided.

Some of the unfriendly people were robbers, lurking for the innocent and unsuspecting travelers so that they could steal from them and kill them. Others would use the cave to hide arms and weapons in order to sell them when the time was ripe for conflict and war. And still others would use the cave for selling slaves. All this made the cave unhappy and furious—so much so that the cave abandoned its welcoming and inviting demeanor.

The cave changed its color from bright and shining white to a dull gray, hoping it would discourage visitors and travelers from seeking shelter in its bosom.

And then one day an even more hideous crime occurred, which made the cave change color again. A seventeen-year-old boy was kidnapped by his brothers because they were jealous of his relationship with their father. They sold their brother to travelers who were on their way to a far distant land. It was when money changed hands that the cave became even more dark and dreary.

As the brothers counted their money, the rains came and the brothers huddled closer together in the back of the cave. But the cave offered no protection or shelter this time. In fact, the cave allowed the ferocious wind to enter and blow all the brothers' money from their hands. With the rain flooding the cave's interior, the money lay in ruins.

Many more years passed with the cave unmoved by humans who occupied its space. But one day the cave had a frightening experience. A man whose notorious reputation was known throughout the entire world came to its bosom to rest and sleep. Goliath was his name. Goliath was a warrior who struck fear in the hearts of people—even the cave trembled. Goliath's anger was so great that one particular day he slammed his fist against the cave and almost brought it crumbling down.

It was this same day that a young boy came face-to-face with Goliath. The young boy was running in fright to the cave, trying to find a weapon to defend himself. The cave made sure a stone from its craggy walls dropped in front of the boy. And when the boy did the impossible, for a split second the cave again became bright white inside. It knew someday the boy would become king of a great nation.

Hundreds of years later, the Lord God Almighty told the cave that the time for the supreme mission that was promised long ago had finally arrived. The cave was not sure what was about to happen but it trusted the Lord God.

One blustery night, a woman and man came seeking shelter after a long trip they had made in haste. As a blanket was sprawled on the ground, the cave realized this wasn't an ordinary couple. The cave made sure that no wind or offensive weather would come in to make it an uncomfortable spot for the birth that was about to take place.

And there were sheep that came, and a cow,
a donkey...
And shepherds...
And angels...
And there was singing...
And there was a hush...
And there was joy!
And the cave knew joy too,
and its colors changed
and the cave became as bright white
as on the day of creation.
And the child smiled...
and the whole world did the same!

■ "People...in darkness have seen...light"

Christmas Eve   **Isaiah 9:1-3; Luke 2:1-14**

Once upon a time, there lived a small community of people in a town so dark and dreary. The children of the community lived in the shadow of their parents' bleak existence. They were taught to be afraid of light because that's the way it had always been.

But the children wanted light. They knew there had to be light. The children asked their parents if it would be possible to bring light into
> their community,
> their homes, and
> their lives.

The parents didn't know how to answer their children. Many parents had no response at all, but there were some who did—and they reacted strongly. Those parents, thinking the children were insulting their intelligence, angrily retorted, "There hasn't been light for hundreds of years! What makes you think there can ever be? Stop questioning us!"

But there were, however, a few parents who encouraged their children to seek out some light, though the parents knew their children's efforts would be fruitless. The children for their part began searching for things that might bring light to their community. One young girl, Katie, caught a lightning bug and wondered if she had the secret to bring light. But her dream was short-lived when it was explained that to breed enough lightning bugs might take a hundred years—and by then she would be an elderly grandmother who wouldn't care anymore.

When all the children learned of Katie's idea, it set off a wild scramble among them. The search for light to brighten the community intensified and brought all the children together working for a cause that everyone— especially their parents—doubted could ever be realized. The search for light not only brought the children together, it also got them working together in harmony which their parents had abandoned ages ago.

One youngster, Evan, found an old flashlight with batteries that amazingly still worked and gave light. But the light was short-lived, and this dampened the spirits of the children. Not to be discouraged, Evan and the others went to a nearby store to buy more batteries, but they were told that batteries had gone out of existence many years ago. Not only were batteries a thing of the past, but the store proprietor told the children that gas and electric light had also been discontinued many years ago because people became frightened of light.

In a chorus, the children asked the inevitable, "Why?" The store owner told the youngsters that light, once shone, tended to show

the flaws of people,
the mistakes of people, and unfortunately,
the sins of people.
The children nonetheless were still eager to find light.

One of the brighter boys, Jason, decided to go to the library before it got too dark so as to find a way to bring light to his community. But his brother, Keith, had another idea. He remembered that when hunting with their dad, he had seen a candle buried in the ground. The boy's father told him that people used to use candles a long time ago but it would be of no use today because people had somehow forgotten how to make candles.

Meanwhile, at the library, the youngster received a message from all the books he was scanning: "Look up." That struck the boy as somewhat odd because the only people who ever looked up to the sky were the children; the adults seldom, if ever, looked up. When this youngster told the other children of the message, Danielle, a bright girl who liked school very much, shared what she had learned in her ancient history class with all the others around her. She said that there was once an abundance of light. Everyone had been happy
to see the sun shine brightly,
to see the moon guide the night,
to see the stars by the millions twinkle, and
to see the clouds bundle together, moving in
unison ever so gracefully.
But then people
began to smoke,
began to pollute,
began to lose values,
began to lose hope,
began to be afraid of light.

It was at that moment that Shane interrupted Danielle saying that light was the people's conscience—and they would rather not deal with it than change any of their habits. He added that "gloom and doom" took over the world—and everyone suffered, even the children. "Look at all the grown-ups," Shane continued.

> "Do they smile?
> do they ever say a kind word?
> do they ever do for anyone except their own?
> do they ever try to share life with others?
> do they want to *enjoy* life?"

Agreeing with what he was hearing, Erik chimed in saying, "Yeah, and light would force people to change their attitudes and the world we all live in; if not, we will always remain unhappy." Joseph, awed by the whole discussion, echoed a rumor that frightened everyone

> whenever,
> wherever

it was spoken. Joseph said that a light was scheduled to pass the earth in a few weeks as it would be completing its journey around the planets. As he was talking, the children became frightened and scared. Coming forward, Desirae, a bright student, urged the youngsters not to be afraid, saying,

> "Light is good for us and the world.
> Light will help us grow and enable us to grow food.
> Light will help us as we travel.
> Light will help us find ourselves! See ourselves!
> Light will warm us and encourage us to love.
> Light will dispel all fears.
> Light will bring us *hope!*"

With a broad smile, Paul, one of the youngest children, said that he wasn't afraid. He said that in a dream he had had a few nights ago, a voice told him

> that light was good,
> that light would make everyone smile.

Another child, Russell, chimed in saying that he wished light would come to our world and stay forever. It was that wish that seemed to ease the fears of all the children. One by one, all the children decided that they would never be afraid of light again; that they would brave all dangers to see that light would be welcome to our world again. A shy Nathan, the youngest child, said that he would do
anything,
everything
to help search for light, adding, "I hope no one does anything that will cause the light to disappear again." All together, the children said they would be willing to dig the ground for the candles that had once been used. Keith called on all the children to come with him to the woods in search of candles. The two oldest knew where they could get shovels and left saying they would be back shortly.

Sometime later the two oldest came back with shovels for everyone. The children enthusiastically went off in search of the candles. Once the children arrived at the site, the digging began. After a few hours and many boxes of candles, stubs and all, the tired and exhausted children realized it was getting too dark to continue or they would miss the light.

All the children gathered on a hill—and waited.
The excitement,
the enthusiasm,
the expectations
were at a fever pitch. The children waited patiently but the adults stayed inside their homes fearful of the event that was about to occur. With no success, the parents tried to lure their children to come in as well. Some of the children began pointing to the west while others were looking eastward. A few were searching the sky overhead.

After some time, a letdown occurred; the children began giving up hope, thinking that the expected light was

really a hoax. But Tony, a severely handicapped
youngster, in the arms of his mom, came up to the hill
where the children had gathered and pointed southward.
And suddenly,
> *The Light came,*
> *shone,*
> *brightened*
>> the night,
>> the hearts of people—all the people.

One by one, the adults came out of their homes to see this
extraordinary Light. The people were reassured that the
Light would be with them forever—and they in turn
vowed never to be afraid of the Light again. It was at this
time that all the children lighted candles for each of the
adults and everyone began to sing "It Came Upon A
Midnight Clear" and other such songs. As they were
singing, all the lights of
> the city
> and
> the world came on!

■ The Resurrection

Easter Sunday (C)   **Acts 10:34; Colossians 3:1; John 20:1**

There was a time in my life that my understanding of The Resurrection Story served a cynical purpose of mine. I often thought The Resurrection Story was the way, or more suspiciously a ploy, to encourage people to live life by certain norms, rules, and regulations.

I thought The Resurrection Story was a nice fairy tale that would entice people
>   to live life fairly and honestly,
>   to live life with respect and honor,
>   to live life by working and striving
>   and saving.

And if our hearts along the way become cold and stony, The Resurrection Promise would mellow and tender our hearts, so as to ensure a nice little world where people who really didn't like one another could somehow live peacefully together. In my mind, it was the social, as well as the Biblical—and to our understanding, Christian, response to the human need of reward and punishment. The concept of the resurrection—long before the teachings of Jesus—ensured an after-life of eternal joy and bliss for

those graduating life with passing grades: while a
resurrection of the damned would be reserved for those
failing life by not measuring up to their full potential. It
would be a life of dismay and misery without end.

What better way to administer this fairy tale, I thought,
than for synagogues, churches, mosques, and temples to
serve as the instrument by which behavior modification
could be enforced—sometimes with dictatorial procession
and power.

That was then
but
this is now.
and this is what I believe:

I believe in the resurrection!

I believe in The Resurrection because
>I believe in Nights—and in Days!
>I believe in the Moon—and in the Sun!
>I believe in the clouds—
>>and the rains they produce!
>I believe in Fall and Winter—
>>in Spring and Summer!

>I believe in all these because
>>I *have seen*—with my very eyes!
>I believe in frost, snow and ice—
>I believe in the water that comes to be...
>I believe in the mustard seed, the smallest of
>>all seeds—
>I believe in the magnificent tree that comes
>>to be...
>I believe in the beach sand that lays around—
>I believe in the crystal that comes to be...
>I believe in the oyster lying in decay—

I believe in the pearl that comes to be...
I believe in coal, the mineral—
I believe in the diamond that comes to be...
I believe in all these because
I *have seen*—with my very eyes!
Folks, what I am trying to proclaim from the pulpit,
is that behind this natural world
of chance and change,
of growth and decay,
where love and hatred live side-by-side, there is
something permanent and perfect which was revealed to
humankind by Jesus' Resurrection—something which all
of us are invited to share.

In our natural world everything that is born must die;
everything has a beginning—and an end. That is why the
Resurrection of all life says something to each one of us:
something about the future—and even beyond the future.
It also says something about our present here and now.
I believe in the God of endless time working
in ancient history and working in our
present age.
I believe in the timid Moses, whose speech
dismayed him—but challenged the
Pharaoh in God's name!
I believe in David, a sinful man of lust
and power, but who in God's name brought
unity to a divided kingdom!
I believe in Peter and Paul—
I believe in God's power working in them,
and the call to discipleship...

And I believe that if the power of God can command
the nights and days,
the moon and the sun,
the clouds and the seasons,
then the power of God can work in us to change us to our
full potential.

I believe that if the power of God can grow the small mustard seed into a magnificent tree, think what the power of God can challenge us to truly be.

I believe if the power of God can change
        sand to crystal,
        coal to diamond,
        oyster shells to pearls,
think what God can accomplish in us in the *here and now*!

I believe if the power of God can raise lilies and tulips from death, think what God can do for our dying faith!

I believe if the power of God can change
        beetles to dragonflies,
        caterpillars to butterflies—
think of the beauty God has instilled in us all that ought to be shared with others.

Jesus with the power of God working in him, transformed the whole of humanity. Jesus is our Resurrection; our call to radically change ourselves for the sake of others: to be disciples for one another so that the kingdom of God can be *seen on earth—as it is in heaven.*

I also believe in a person who saw absolutely no meaning in his life—and now I believe in the meaning of *all* people's lives—including *my own.*

Why shouldn't I believe in the resurrection?

After *seeing* the greatness God has given each of you— and constantly raising each of you up to accomplish great potential: *Why shouldn't you believe in the resurrection?!*

■ The Meaning of Ashes in Lent

Ash Wednesday   **Joel 2:12-18; Matthew 6:1-6,16-18**

Tree Planting: A Skit for Children

Narrator: It's a beautiful, spring day, late one Saturday morning. Harry, Lee, and Mary are waiting for their friend, Nick.

Mary: I wonder where Nick is?

Lee: Yes, if he doesn't get here soon, we'll miss soccer practice and the game this afternoon.

Harry: Mom and I drove past Nick's house earlier this morning. I saw a really big hole in his side yard. I hope nothing's wrong.

Mary: Look! Here comes Nick now.

Lee: What's that he's got with him?

Harry: It looks like a wheelbarrow. Let's find out what's up.

All three: Hey, Nick. Hurry up!

Nick: Hi guys. What's going on?

Mary: That's what we want to know. What's with the wheelbarrow? We've got to practice for the soccer game this afternoon.

Lee: What's all that dirt for? I don't ever remember seeing dirt that black before.

Harry: Where are you going with it?

Nick: Hold up now. I'll still be able to make it to the game, but I've got to help my dad first. I'm helping my dad plant an apple tree in our side yard. I got this dirt from my grandpa's house. He burned a bunch of leaves and twigs and saved the ashes for us.

Mary: Now wait a minute Nick. What's ashes got to do with planting a tree? After all, ashes aren't anything but dead burned things.

Lee: Oh, I get it! When you mix ashes with dirt, you're really making the soil richer by putting more nutrients into it.

Nick: That's right, Lee. It's almost like when your mom gives you a vitamin pill. But this time we're using something that has died to help bring new life and help nurture it.

Harry: Wow, Nick! Do you know what that sounds like? It sounds like what our priest was telling us about Jesus. He loved us so much that he died on a cross for us. And, they buried him in a cut-out rock. When he rose up from the dead, he gave us new life.

Nick: That's right, Harry. It's for that reason that we get ashes on Ash Wednesday. The ashes symbolize our death and our rising to new life with Jesus.

Mary: Just out of curiosity, why's your dad planting an apple tree instead of a rosebush, for instance?

Harry: Yea, roses are prettier to look at than apples.

Nick: We're planting a tree for lots of reasons. Once it fills out a little, we can sit under it for shade. And when it's grown for several years, it'll help shade the house. Besides, my whole family likes apples: they're good food.

Lee: You know, once the branches fill out and get sturdy, birds will probably make their homes in your tree. You might even get some of the squirrels I've seen in the area.

Nick: That's what my folks are hoping for. Mom says we should all do our parts to help take care of God's creatures.

Harry: I guess you're better off planting a tree. Trees give us lumber to build houses and furniture. We get pencils and toothpicks from trees, too.

Mary: You know they take little pieces of wood and grind them up to make pulp. When you mix it with water, you can make paper.

Lee: Remember what we learned in science class. The green leaves use the sunlight and water to breathe in a lot of bad air. Then, the leaves breathe out oxygen, which all humans and animals need to live.

Nick: I think a tree just might be the best plant God ever created. Besides, if you've ever just laid down under a tree and looked up at its branches, you'd be truly amazed at how beautiful the detail is. Look guys, I've really got to get going. My dad's waiting for this load of soil and ashes. But don't worry about the soccer game. I'll make it the about your tree has really gotten me interested in your project. Do you think I could help you plant your tree?

Mary: Can I help, too?

Nick: I don't think Dad will mind. He could probably use the extra help.

Lee: I'll help too! Here, let me carry your shovel for you.

■ In the Breaking of the Bread

3rd Sunday of Easter (B)   **Luke 24:35-48**

I find it very interesting that the call of the disciples
began on the shore of a lake as the future disciples were
hauling in fish. I can imagine there must have been times
when some of the fish they caught were cooked right there
on the sand as they celebrated the fruits of their labor.

Meals were very important in the time of Jesus. Remember
    the five barley loaves and the two fishes,
    the marriage feast of Cana,
    the feeding of the four thousand and then the
      five thousand,
    the host inviting everyone to his banquet, and
    Lazarus at the table of the rich man?

One could also include
    the sinful woman dining at the Pharisee
      Simon's house,
    supper with Martha and Mary,
    the feast at the return of the "Lost Son,"
    the dinner invitation to the home of
    Zacchaeus, the tax collector, and even

Jesus and his disciples eating grain against
the protests of the Pharisees.
The parables of Jesus included many examples or
allusions to food such as:
the sower,
the seed,
the leaven,
the yeast.

It is after a meal that Jesus asks Peter if his impetuous
disciple truly loves him. When Peter bares his soul to the
Lord, Jesus shares with him the toll that discipleship
would require.

However, the greatest meal of Jesus' was his last.
Realizing that his death was near, Jesus asked his
disciples to remember this meal just as the Jewish people
continued to remember the One God working through the
ages in a similar meal at Passover.

After the resurrection, Jesus continued to stress the
importance of meal celebration. Appearing to his disciples
on numerous occasions, Jesus, though different, yet the
same, sat and ate in their company. I find it intriguing
that at the end of John's gospel, that is, after the
resurrection, Jesus is found at the seashore awaiting the
disciples to bring ashore their haul. There is the Master,
overseeing a charcoal fire with fish and bread cooking—
preparing for a meal.

In our own time, as we eat of the bread of Jesus, each of
us is going to be challenged to love and forgive as never
before. And in that love and forgiveness, we are to give of
ourselves for others. It is in this transformation of the
bread, that we can become like Jesus, and can become
Jesus for others.

Sometimes, in the breaking of the bread, we see that our behavior in life needs some alterations. I experienced this in my teens. I grew up in an area of Philadelphia called Rhawnhurst, where there were as many Jewish people as there were Catholics. There were about 100,000 people in this area and eighty percent were either Catholic or Jewish.

In my teenage years I belonged to a street gang that hung out in front of a delicatessen owned by a middle-aged couple who were Jewish. All of us hanging on the street corner were "very" Catholic even though we did not practice our faith or were very knowledgeable in it. We were young toughs who had strong dislikes and hatreds. Prominent on our hate lists were Jews ("Kikes," as we called them) and Blacks (or "niggers," as we called them), even though we seldom had any real experiences with them since they didn't live in our neighborhood.

There may have been rougher areas in the city, but we felt we could handle anything that would come our way. One of the things we did well was to taunt the Jewish youths whenever we saw them pass our corner. Seeing their fear gave us a great deal of pleasure. All the while, the Jewish couple who ran the delicatessen heard and saw how we threatened and harassed Jews who passed by. I suppose we did what we did to the Jews because they believed and acted differently than we did. We had so stereotyped the Jews of the neighborhood that nothing they did could ever change our attitudes toward them.

Even though our gang would always eat in the deli, I never gave it a thought that the Jewish couple who ran it had strong feelings about our behavior toward their people that were deeply hidden inside them. But one day I said "kike" once too often and Sol, the owner of the deli, grabbed me by my shirt collar, pinned me to a table and told me, "You pray to my God...and remember that Jesus was a Jew."

I couldn't begin to explain my humiliation and embarrassment that no one from my corner stepped forward to assist me, a normal thing we did for one another. Everyone saw and heard yet made no move, a moment frozen in time. For at that one moment, truth challenged our attitude. I didn't know what to say and left the deli to the cheers of some of the older customers.

For as long as we stayed on that corner, I seldom again went inside that deli. My embarrassment was too strong. I felt intimidated even thinking of what happened that day, knowing it would always be with me. Yet, there was something inside me that really wanted to understand this experience more deeply. At the time, I didn't have the nerve to inquire and life went on. As we grew older, hanging at our "corner" changed to hanging in a neighborhood bar. Yet, I could never seem to forget that one moment in my life. I was haunted by it and wanted it resolved in my life, but I didn't know how to do it without my pride being hurt.

Years later while I was attending college in up-state Pennsylvania, I came back to that deli. Sol was still there and I asked him if he would like to share a hoagie with me. Sol gladly accepted. We shared our thoughts about that day several years before as if it had only been a few days ago. As Sol spoke, I found myself listening to a profound person who had a great respect for his faith and the faith of others. As he spoke, I realized that what I had done in my younger years was behavior that hit at the very heart of a people's identity. After our meal together, I found that I had gained a greater respect for Sol and, more importantly, for the Jewish people.

It was in the breaking of the bread that His disciples recognized that Jesus was truly The Messiah: alive and well! So it was when Sol and I ate together that day. We discovered each other in new ways. I learned about Sol and the Jewish people, and Sol came to understand how I had struggled for years to reconcile my actions of the past and how I could now change.

Each of us who eats of the Bread must change. We must be for one another and be transformed into the likeness of Jesus for all to see. In doing that, people will recognize the Lord Jesus through us.

■ The Good Shepherd

4th Sunday of Easter (B)   **John 10:11-18**

We've all heard the story of the Good Shepherd. But, did you realize that there are two versions?

In today's Gospel reading, we have John's account of the sheep following the Master's voice and of the shepherd laying down his life for his own.

In Luke's account of the Good Shepherd we find a marked contrast, as the author gives his readers a different perspective. In this account, we find a sheep that loses its way and a shepherd who leaves the rest of the flock in search. When the shepherd finds the stray sheep, a celebration takes place; the one that was lost has been found. This story of the lost sheep then leads to the story of the woman who finds the lost coin and to the famous story of the prodigal son who, after living a life of foolishness and sin in a distant country, is welcomed home. Luke, in his story of the lost sheep, wanted to focus on the love of a Master who is willing to do anything to rescue the lost one just like a true shepherd would do for the sheep in his care.

In John's gospel account, however, it appears that the responsibility rests on both the shepherd and the sheep. If the good shepherd is to lead, the sheep will have to do their part by recognizing the shepherd's voice and following his lead.

In our own lives, we need to recognize the Master's voice and to follow his Word as best we can. Jesus has done his part. Our lives should reflect that our Shepherd is Jesus and our responsibility is to follow him with all our hearts despite any false leaders in our midst.

Sheep are not the smartest animals around. In fact they are considered to be pretty dumb. Many times, we also do very stupid things and we need the love that Luke and John have illustrated in their gospels of the Good Shepherd. Sometimes our foolish actions have consequences that allow us to experience change in ourselves and to become smarter. Something like that happened when I was about thirteen years old. I was in the eighth grade, at the time, acting very immature, as cocky and brazen as can be. Though and nasty because I was lacking in self-worth, had low
self-esteem, and little
self-confidence.

As it turned out I sat in my eighth grade class next to the prettiest girl in the world. I felt so lucky to be so close to her, but she never gave me so much as a friendly look. Though I did some awful things hoping to grab her attention and admiration, they all failed due to my stupid and erroneous belief that acting tough and nasty was the way to win her attention.

I was infatuated with her. I yearned to ask her out, but I hesitated because of my belief that I was the homeliest guy in the world. I mean to say that with all my pimples, with all my awkward gestures, my shyness, my stuttering, my messed-up hair, I couldn't even like myself let alone others, especially Barbara. "So why should she go out with me?", I asked myself over and over again. But the desire to ask Barbara out was even stronger. Then one day despite all that I believed about myself, and all my insecurities, I found the courage to ask "Barbara, would you like to go out with me?" She answered, "No!" I never felt so crushed in my life! I felt depressed and rejected for months thereafter.

But my yearning to date Barbara never left me. We, again, found ourselves sitting next to each other in high school. As always, she was very cool to me, never so much as to give a smile. Still hoping someday to date her, I watched to see the kind of guys she would go out with, so that I might imitate them and gain her favor.

The first guy I observed was a weightlifter. He had muscles everywhere! And Oh, was he strong. So I figured that what I ought to do was to be a weightlifter. I borrowed some weights from a friend of mine and practiced, hoping my skinny and scrawny body would develop into something that would be magnificent. I tried for several weeks but to no avail. I felt I was meant to be skinny and gave up. It was about that same time that Barbara ditched this weightlifter and started dating the most popular boy in school. This guy was involved in nearly every club the school had to offer. From that, I gathered his attraction must be his personality. So, just to win Barbara's heart, I joined many of the same clubs that this second fellow was a member of. But soon I realized that this wasn't my style. I felt out of step, and I realized his style wasn't for me even if it meant that Barbara would never go out with me. But alas, he was dumped too.

Finally, it was a bookworm that Barbara started dating. "That's it!" I thought. "I ought to be hitting the books and perhaps be a brain and maybe Barbara would go out with me." Now I must admit that I never did homework in my life up to this point. Never did I ever so much as open a book! But I was willing to try just to have a shot at Barbara. But that was short-lived. It lasted only a week. I just couldn't get myself to do it. Anyway, I thought she wasn't *that good* and gave up any hopes of dating Barbara.

It was some twenty years later that I happened to bump into Barbara on a Philadelphia subway. I had heard she had married many years before. Barbara and I recognized each other, and after some pleasantries, I asked her whom she married. She said, "Andy." "*Andy?*" I couldn't help but repeat what she said. Now I knew Andy, and if I thought I was the homeliest guy around, I *knew* Andy was! I just *knew* I was better looking than Andy.

After the shock wore off, I wanted to know what attracted Barbara to Andy. What Barbara told me has stayed with me to this day. "I married him," she said, "because he was nice and had a great deal of compassion and love." That was it! Compassion and love; not tough and nasty and being a wiseguy. I recognized now those are the important things in life.

John reminds us of the same thing. John tells us that we ought to recognize Jesus as the Shepherd who leads us on the right path in life. And if we follow his teachings, we will win the right to come home to him.

In knowing the Shepherd Jesus, we will understand the value and goodness of our own being and will not be led astray by those who compete with him. They know not what the flock is all about or how to respect the dignity of others. So each of us needs to be a smart sheep who is full of integrity and who will continue to follow Jesus and be a true disciple.

■ "I know not how to speak"

4th Sunday of Ordinary Time (C)   **Jeremiah 1:4-10,17-19;**
Luke 4:1-30

When I was about five years old I realized I had an
impediment: I was a stutterer. I remember everyone
telling me to
> slow down,
> take a deep breath,
> think before speaking,
> listen to what you're saying.

The more people told me these kinds of things, the more I
became apprehensive about opening my mouth. At first,
my stuttering was a nuisance to me and those around me.
But as it became more pronounced, it became a major
problem for me.

Like the time when I was living in the orphanage and
Sister What-ever-her-name-was had all the kids who had
beds in the dorm (about a hundred) come and kneel by my
bed and pray that I would begin speaking right. I recall
Sister What-ever-her-name-was putting a relic of a saint
on my throat so that my stuttering would be healed. It
never did the trick. In fact, my stuttering got worse!

As I entered my teenage years, my stuttering was atrocious. I wasn't just a cute little kid anymore; I was an embarrassment to myself. It prompted many unkind remarks and crude laughter, not only from my peers, but from total strangers. If you have ever met someone who stuttered, you can appreciate what I went through. People's laughter hurt me deep inside. After all, it wasn't my fault if I stuttered. I felt terrible about myself. Whatever self-image or self-esteem, or self worth I had, and that was important to me, was evaporated each time I would open my mouth. But worst yet, I would hold all that anger and resentment inside me until there was an opening when I threw a temper tantrum at anyone who would so much as smile while I was trying to say something. The worse part of it was that my temper was not just aimed at those whom I perceived were "making fun of me," but at anyone, just anyone at all.

All that pent-up anger that was festering inside, attacked an unsuspecting someone without any apparent cause. That's what happens when someone without self-worth thinks others are poking fun at him.

I carried this stigma with me into my twenties. By that time, I realized that certain things were happening. For one thing, though all the letters of the alphabet were problematic for me, often causing me to stutter as much as ten minutes, the one letter of the alphabet that caused me the most problems was the letter S. I could not begin a sentence that started with the letter S in less than fifteen minutes, usually with much embarrassment (and horror) within myself and a great deal of amusement for those speaking with me. It was about this time that I began to frequent a neighborhood bar with a few of my friends. I wanted to enjoy the company of my friends but I could never have a couple of beers with them without having to leave the establish with feelings of anger and frustration.

You see, at this bar they only had three beers on tap. The beers were Schmidt's, Schlitz, and Schafer! No wonder I couldn't spend time spent with my friends. It would take forever for me to order—and oh, how those people would laugh at my expense. I made a point that that would never happen to me again.

As it happened, I saw a column in the newspaper stating that there was a sure way for stutterers to overcome their impediment. It was to look at the mirror every morning and evening and say a word that was most problematic a thousand times. This would continue for about two weeks as the article stated, "...all your fears will vanish in a second." I thought about that and decided to give it a try. But I wanted to be a bit clever about it. Though my friends seldom drank bottle beer, I decided to forgo the usual tap beers of Schmidt's, Schlitz, and Schafer and cut the name of a bottled beer down to "Bud." "That's it!" I said to myself. "I'll show them."

For the next three weeks I looked at the mirror, morning and night, saying a thousand times each time "Bud." When I felt supremely confident about my ability to say "Bud" with out a single stutter, I headed to the bar with my friends. After they ordered the usual, I said to the bartender "Bud." "Sorry," he said, "we're out of Bud. We only have Schmidt's, Schlitz, and Schafer." Believe me, I was demoralized.

Today I speak fine. There was a person in my life who believed when he came to the altar to receive the bread of Jesus, he *had* to be Jesus. Because he made that his mission, he went a step beyond what his professional duties required.

Speaking is essential to getting the Word out.

Jeremiah, like other prophets of old—or the present—had
flaws in his own person and ability.
> "I know not how to speak;
> I am too young,"
Jeremiah protested to the Lord.

But the Lord had a different message: "To whomever I
send you, you shall go; whatever I command you, you
shall speak." When the Lord touched the mouth of the
future and great prophet with a tender hand. It was
evident that the Word from the mouth of the prophet
Jeremiah—and any prophet—had the mission of
> rooting up,
> tearing down,
> destroying,
> demolishing—
all in order
> to build,
> to plant.

When Jesus spoke in the synagogue, scripture tells us
that those present "marveled at the appealing discourse
which came from his lips." But that was short-lived. As
with Jeremiah, and all prophets, the Words, though
blessed, became a bark that people would rather quiet
down than take in. The Words of Jesus were quickly
dismissed when they called for people to change and
transform themselves and their society. But The Prophet
was not even accepted in his native place. The
townspeople even intended to hurl Jesus over the edge of
a cliff—but The Prophet went straight through their
midst and walked away.

In many respects I can identify with Jeremiah and any
prophets whose Words weren't accepted.

In Jeremiah's case, maybe the confidence God placed in him was the catalyst that enabled him to withstand public humiliation, arrest, confinement, and finally exile, and yet be remembered for his Words forever.

In my case, it was because of someone's confidence in the power of God, and in the ability of people, unsuspecting people, to overcome the difficulties of life and be people able to speak the Word.

■ "Your sins are forgiven"

7th Sunday of Ordinary Time (B)   **Mark 2:1-12**

Aside from calling God
        his Father,
        his Daddy,
what brought Jesus the disapproval of those in power was
the claim that he had the *authority* to forgive sins. The
leaders of the people took great exception to that kind of
talk. "Why does the man talk in that way?" they asked
each other. If they, the Scribes and the Pharisees, could
not forgive sins with all their "respectability," then no one
should—and mustn't. Only God can do that—and they
knew God wasn't around, at all.

But if Jesus wanted to come to Capernaum, drawing
many of its citizens to his teachings, and heal the lepers
and the paralyzed, that was perfectly fine with them. "As
long as the preacher frees the ill from their infirmities and
maladies," said the leaders as they conspired among
themselves. "It would only serve our purpose." The Scribes
and Pharisees knew they couldn't heal the sick but they
were in business when it came to sin. The leaders knew

the people lived constantly in guilt about their sins and through the power they wielded, these leaders wanted their presence to be made known and respected.

Jesus, on the other hand, was
>different;
>extremely different,
>incredibly different!

Jesus came not only to heal those afflicted with various ailments, but also those afflicted with sin. Jesus knew that he was courting danger. Once he began to forgive sins, he knew
>the controversies,
>the conflicts,
>the rumors,
>the scrutinizing
would never end—even if he were to die!

To Jesus, the ultimate mission of his life was to say to those in sin, "I absolve you from your sins, now go in peace." And that was the end of it. No need to recall or to remember the sins that were forgiven. A clean slate, if you will. The Scribes and the Pharisees would have none of it.

As I reflect on my own life, I remember I always felt good when I left things—those things that had caused me embarrassment or shame—behind. That is what God does for each of us.

I remember hanging on the street corner with plenty of company back in the early sixties. Everyone was a tough guy—if for no other reason than by the identity of the gang. But there was one guy who was respected by everyone on the corner. His name was Bartholomew Albert Dwyer. You would think he would want to be called Bart
>or Barry,
>maybe Bar,
>or even Al.

But no, Bartholomew Albert Dwyer wanted to be called B.A.D. So we called him BAD. After all, he was six feet six and weighed two hundred and thirty pounds. And he was still growing at the young age of seventeen! BAD was by far the roughest guy on the corner. When he laughed, we all laughed. When he was upset, we were all upset. It was what I would call, the "Al Capone syndrome." I especially remember when BAD fell in love with a girl named Susie. That's all we heard for months, "Susie this", and "Susie that." Though we guys on the corner never saw Susie, she must have been a great catch because BAD never stopped talking about her. He drove us all crazy, every night on the corner, "Susie this," "Suse that."

That kind of infatuation led BAD to a tattoo joint one day. One might think that tattoos would have been very common among the members of a corner gang. Actually, very few of us ever considered having one. But BAD was so much "in love" with Susie that he came to the corner one night after having almost his whole body covered with tattoos—all having to do with, of course, Susie.

> Hearts,
> flowers,
> ships,
> slogans—

all pertaining to Susie. Of course, we all told BAD that it was a great idea, although we all felt BAD had fallen overboard with "the love of his life."

That "love affair" came to a screeching halt one night when BAD found out that Susie was two-timing him. BAD had it out with the guy, poor fella. As for Susie, we really never heard. BAD would come to the corner and his moods would swing like a pendulum; from extreme hurt and rejection to great anger and embarrassment. It lasted for many months. We all did our part coping with BAD.

Eventually BAD met other girls and developed a more mature relationship with them, and he became a much happier person—but it all took precious time.

I haven't seen BAD in many years. I do know, however, that BAD is a "Philadelphia lawyer" and is married to a girl by the name of Sharon. But I suspect that BAD, try as he might, will never wholly forget his experience with Susie.

The lesson of Jesus is quite simple: his forgiveness is forgiveness. We need not revisit our sinfulness and relive it. All we really need to know is that Jesus heals and restores us to his relationship with his Father. In believing Jesus, we learn from our sinful moments and chances are we won't fall
> in the same way,
> in the same sin, again.

Neither God nor Jesus will remind us!

■ "Are you the King of the Jews?"

Christe the King (B)   **John 18:33-37**

I'd like to take you on a trip back to "yesteryear,"
      when the TV age was but an infant,
      when
            The Lone Ranger,
            I Love Lucy,
            Red Skelton,
            Milton Berle,
            Jackie Gleason,
            Bishop Sheen,
            Ed Sullivan,
            Dinah Shore, and
            Dave Garraway
were household names.

Popular, also, were game shows. Shows like
            Twenty-One,
            Tic-Tac-Dough,
            Sixty-Four Thousand Dollar Question,
            Name That Tune, and
            The Price Is Right.

The one show I remember the most was *Queen for a Day.*
The show's MC was Jack Bailey. It was one of the first
shows of its kind that invited audience participation. This
was done by having two women contestants share their
stories of heartbreak and misery,
stories of wishes that would help satisfy their
particular needs.

The contestants were to compete against one another to
capture the hearts and souls of the audience. It was the
audience that would determine the value and worth of the
stories that were told. Jack Bailey was, in essence, the
king who would lavish the winner with an array of gifts
and merchandise that would transform a helpless, tearful
housewife and give her her fondest wish.

Even in these days of "yesteryear," ratings were
important. I don't know for sure, but I would guess that,
even though the show was seen in the late afternoon, it
captured just as large an audience as Milton Berle and Ed
Sullivan in their heydays. In order to preserve its ratings,
the show's contestants had to outdo one another. It went
something like this:

1st Contestant

> My husband was involved with the local Junior
> Achievement. One night while on his way to pick up
> some youths, his car was hit head on and he was left
> paralyzed from the waist down, leaving me and my
> four children with very little to depend on...

By this time tears were flowing from everyone in the
audience. The audience was then asked to applaud based
on the woman's testimony. Over the television screen one
would see a monitor showing the numbers one to a
hundred. If the story was compelling enough, the needle
on the monitor would hit a certain number, say 85

indicating fairly good response. After which the second contestant would then share her story:

2nd Contestant

> My son was born with polio and we are struggling
> with six other children in a house that lacks a washer
> and dryer. My husband works two jobs and he is
> unable to buy these machines, for all his wages feed
> our children...

Again, as with the first contestant, Jack Bailey invited the audience to show their support—and again, the monitor's needle reached a number indicative of the effectiveness of the contestant's story.

At the end, one contestant was declared the winner. The winner was
> showered with
> a crown,
> a robe,
> placed on a throne, and
> given roses

proclaiming her
> "Queen,"
> "Queen for a Day."

Gifts of every kind were presented to the now-smiling "Queen":
> vacuum cleaners,
> refrigerators,
> freezers,
> televisions,
> ovens
> even trips to Rome and Paris.

Her every wish came true.

Today we celebrate the Feast of Christ the King. We
reaffirm that Jesus is indeed a king. But a king
    so different,
    so extraordinary,
that his kingship claims his life.

Pilate questions Jesus: "Are you the King of the Jews?"
Jesus' first response is indirect, an appeal to Pilate's
conscience. Pilate has to make a decision. There is, after
all, a Jewish audience watching his every move. There is
also a Roman audience that is watching as well. Pilate
wants Jesus to tell his story, hoping his story will take
him off the hook, but Jesus is not falling for it. Pilate has
to make his own determination. He again questions Jesus,
"Your own nation [has] handed you over to me." Again,
Pilate questions "Then you are a king?" Jesus' second
response is crisp and to the point: "My kingdom does not
belong to this world." A strikingly different king!

Jesus then looks to his audience and says:
    "I was born to testify to the truth.
      I will tell you what my kingship has done,
        and if you have heard me and believed me,
        you can give testimony on my behalf.
      I have proclaimed the Good News
        of my Father;
      I have cured every disease and illness
        that afflicts your people;
      I have spent time with your lame,
        your lunatics, your paralyzed,
        and I have loved them;
      I have rejoiced with your children;
      I have mourned for your dead;
      I have even raised your dead to life again;
      I have eaten with
        your sinners,
        your tax collectors,

your deceitful religious,
your wicked politicians—
and gave them a change of heart,
and you wanted to make me a king.
But then I told you to be the light
of the world.

When I told you not to break the
commandments and teach others not to,
When I told you not to place yourself above
others,
When I told you not to insult and hurt one
another,
When I told you not to be judgmental toward
others,
When I told you not to retaliate,
When I told you not to be hypocrites,
When I told you not to be hooked on material
things,
When I told you to love one another,
When I told you to love your enemies,
When I told you to respect women—
and not give in to lust,
When I told you to look at your own sins and
faults,
When I told you to pray with a sincere heart,
When I told you to wash each other's feet
in service—and do for others,
When I told you to pray for those who hurt
you,
When I told you to do to others what you
would have them do to you,
When I told you you must forgive,
you took away my kingship and agreed
to my arrest and trial.

But even at this late date,
    I forgive you;
    I love you;
    I still want you to follow me;
    I still have power to heal all your diseases
       and illnesses;
    I still have power to raise your dead;
    I still have power to give new life;
    I have the power to judge.

Now, what is your verdict?

Pilate left—in silence. But the audience shouted:
    "Crucify him!"
    "Crucify him!"
    "Crucify him!"
The needle of the monitor must have been close to a
hundred.

You, our audience, decide: Is Jesus king, just for a day?

■ Too much pride to sin?

11th Sunday of Ordinary Time (C)   **2 Samuel 12:7-10**
                                              Luke 7:36-50

Recently I went to visit an eighty-year-old lady in the
hospital. She was suffering from terminal cancer.
Normally, visiting people in the hospital becomes routine
for a priest. But this visit was something to write about.
This was because of the person in question and what she
really thought about herself.

Being eighty years old hadn't take away her charm and
pride. Especially her pride in herself and the way she
looked and dressed. Even in her pain,
              her obvious loss of weight,
              her stark paleness,
she wanted to dress in her finest. Though she couldn't
wear any of her beautiful clothes, she wore a robe that
must have been purchased from Bloomingdales or
Nordstroms. She had made sure her hair was properly
combed and that her lips had the right shade of lipstick.

But all that aside, this eighty-year-old lady had a major
concern. It was not that she was afraid of dying, though
she was. Her main concern was: "What's going to happen

when I die?" Pondering how I should respond to her question, I sensed she wanted to know everything that happens when death comes, especially, how she was going to be judged for her actions in this life. I got an even greater sense that this frail lady was afraid because of her sins; though, I'm sure, in her lifetime she would have been too proud to admit her wrongs. Now, she wanted to know, "What's going to happen to me?"

I told her that I'd read many books on "near death" experiences and before I could finish my sentence she interrupted, "Tell me! I want to know!" I shared that it was my belief that when death comes we'll be able to feel ourselves leaving our body, and hover over it, knowing that the pain that was part of that body will never touch us again. I continued to explain that somehow we would pass through concrete walls and ceilings and enter a black hole or tunnel, traveling trillions and trillions of miles per hour, or so it would seem. We would not be hampered by any sort of time, space, and boundaries. Finally, we would see, at the end of that black tunnel, a bright light that would give us all the peace and love we could ever imagine on earth. That sense of peace and love would be so awesome that we would know it is our Creator. Again, the frail lady interrupted me, "What about purgatory?" Ha! The real reason she was so concerned, I thought.

Though I didn't want to overwhelm her, I continued with my understanding of the death experience—and let the chips fall as they may. I told her that a "Being of All Light" would go through the events of our lives with us: the good and the bad. I shared with her that in the review of our lives, the pain and hurt we caused others would come back to us. Her eyes squinted. But I calmed her when I said that that "Being of Light" would be with us to comfort us even as we were experiencing the effects of our life decisions.

However, the frail woman's calm didn't last very long. Putting her slightly trembling hand to her mouth, the woman whispered to me, "I'm in trouble." She told me that her sins were many, and she had much to answer for. I immediately tried to calm her fears, for I was touching a weak, almost helpless woman whom I couldn't ever imagine having done anything to hurt anyone. I told her honestly that I had more to answer for than she, for I knew I had hurt people with "my Italian temper." Interrupting me once again, she said, "No, my Irish temper has inflicted pain on many people, which I regret."

What was extraordinary about this exchange was the fact that this frail lady was even able to admit to her sins. She was a proud woman who gave the impression in her latter years of being gentle, although I don't think too many people were fooled. Nonetheless, at this late date, she came to terms with her faults and sins. After sharing with me some moments in her life that were not wonderful examples of being a Christian, we both held hands, laughed, and celebrated the fact that Jesus came to heal fallen people like ourselves who knew that we had indeed failed.

Pride is a part of all of us: the best—and the not so best. Sometimes even the best fail; while the least pass the test of overcoming that pride that will come back to torment us.

In Luke's Gospel, Simon the Pharisee had Jesus over for dinner. While at the dining table, a certain woman with a seamy reputation came and interrupted their eating and began to wash the Master's feet with compassion. That humble act, a rather embarrassing act I would suppose, gained her the forgiveness of the Lord. Simon, was quite perturbed by this interruption, and immediately passed judgment, not only on the woman with the seamy reputation but on Jesus as well. Simon, it is shown, was too full of pride to give to Jesus what was needed so he could be healed of his own sinfulness. Simon, using the parlance of our times, just didn't get it!

On the other hand, David, the king of the land of Israel, was a calculating and manipulative womanizer, who stole someone's wife and ordered the death of her husband, thereby allowing him to marry her and father a child. God sent Nathan the prophet to challenge the king for his sins. Nathan did this by sharing a story with David that brought a response of outrage from the king. When the prophet confronted David with the fact that the scoundrel in his story was none other than the king himself, David was filled with remorse. Again, using the parlance of our times, David got the picture, the full picture!

No sin,

> not the woman with the seamy reputation,
> not David with his murderous adultery,
> not even Simon with all his pride

is greater than the love of God. All we need to do is

> realize our faults,
> acknowledge the hurt to ourselves
> > and others,
> renew ourselves to a different path in life—

and forgiveness will be gladly given by the love of our Creator.

The frail woman is still alive at this book's publication. Only her fear is dead!

For she knows forgiveness!

■ "The Empty Tomb"

What must have been the disciples' reaction to the empty
tomb? None of the four gospel writers expressed the
disciples' reaction in quite the same way. It must have
been a totally disturbing, empty feeling.
>   Did all their hopes collapse?
>   Did all faith die?
After traveling
>   with him, after receiving all those
>   reassurances
>   from him
>   about his relationship with the Father, and
>   the calamity of Friday,
>   the stillness of Saturday, and
>   the reality of Sunday morning
made the disciples realize that they were all alone.

Those words of his, "after three days, the Son of Man will
arise from the dead," must have been a far distant
memory; must have seemed like a cruel hoax to them.
And so these confused disciples were hiding in a building
far away

from the hustle and bustle
of the festivities in the Holy City;
   locked in a room all by themselves,
   insecure in their state of
      fright,
      fear, and
      trepidation—
all of a sudden they open the door to a familiar knock and
the disciples hear:
      "The tomb is empty!
      The body is gone!
      They've taken the body!"

At that moment, nothing mattered but the apparent
confirmed loss of him who led them. But they had to see
for themselves. Two of the disciples went to the tomb and
the confirmation was official: "They've taken the body and
buried it in another place"—
      "They" being the religious culprits who
         wouldn't want a shrine for a blasphemer;
      "They" being the government who surely
         didn't want people flocking to the tomb
         of a revolutionist.

The two disciples came and gave their eyewitness report
to the others. Their faces reflected a total sense of
      dejection,
      rejection.

Now the empty tomb is not peculiar to Jesus. We all have
to face empty tombs. Many of us have already experienced
empty tombs in our lives. That is to say, we have been
confronted
      empty hearts,
      empty hopes,
      empty faith,
      empty spirits.

My particular empty tomb occurred a few years ago when
a friend and I went to the very source of my early identity:
the orphanage where I was reared. Easter, 1983, was the
occasion of this sentimental trip back in time. I was
hoping to recapture the noisy experience twenty-five years
to the day I left.

I never remembered a day in the orphanage when noise
was not heard. Noise was *essential* to
> the life,
> the soul,
> the heart

of our
> coming together,
> growing in maturity,
> learning to care for one another.

My empty tomb was the empty orphanage:
> No children,
> No games,
> No playing,
> No catching,
> No swimming,
> No running,
> No screaming,
> No crying,
> No laughing,
> No smiling faces.

All I saw were badly run-down and deteriorating
buildings, wild weeds covering the vast playground, and
graffiti plastered on every wall. Those once-used
> swings,
> monkeybars, and the
> hopscotch board

were motionless, dead where they stood.

I couldn't stay. The source that provided me with so much
life was now unable to provide me with even a ray of hope.
I left shattered, with a feeling of emptiness.

I realize today what the disciples had gone through.
Seeing the vitality of *who they were* being
        slain,
        buried, and
        taken away from them forever.
A really dismal feeling of helplessness.

But what I know today—and what the disciples found out
that first Easter, is the importance of not the place—
be it the tomb or the orphanage—but the hope in the
potential of *the* experience; the hope in the potential
        of the human family,
        of the human being because
          of him who lived with us for a little while,
          and
          of him who lives in our hearts
            forevermore—if we allow him to.

■ John the Baptist

There were crowds of people
                    coming to the Jordan River,
                    coming because of all the commotion
                    John the Baptist was creating.
The Baptist was baptizing the many who approached him
with the intention of giving up their old way of living.

John was also challenging others in the throngs who were
not approaching and urging them to be more faith-filled
people.

Many coming to the Jordan were people who had never
believed in very many things; people who were always
suspicious of anything that had to do with
                    belief,
                    commitment, and
                    transformation.

                    While John was baptizing,
                    while John was making the straight path for
                        the one who was to come,

the many in the multitudes came up to the Baptizer and
pointedly asked him,
>"Are you he who is to come?
>Are you the Messiah?"

The Baptizer was startled.

He stepped back a few steps.

He hesitated for a few seconds—and in those few short
moments, the Baptizer took a good look
>at himself,
>within himself,
and knew what to say. He said boldly, "No,
>I am not he who is to come.
>I am not the Messiah.
>I am not holy enough to untie
>>his sandal straps."

Many
>did not understand,
>could not comprehend,
>would not allow John's message to sink in.

>"But then, who are you?
>Are you Elijah?
>Are you Isaiah?"

"No," said the Baptizer, "I'm neither. I am a voice in the
wind." The crowds were upset, for ever since their
childhood they had been told that a Messiah was coming.
Before their very eyes stood someone who was preparing
the way—and all they could see of him was
>a man in camel-hair clothing,
>a man living in the wilderness,
>a man talking of some sort of repentance.

"Where then is this man you talk so much about?" the answer-hungry crowd wanted to know. The Baptizer charged them, "Be prepared, reform, for the time is at hand."

The crowds kept pressing the Baptizer, nonetheless. "Where is he who is to come?" And John shouted, "You will surely know the Messiah when he walks along side you."

Now some of these were impulsive folks, sent by desperate people who were concerned with
        their status,
        their selfish style of living,
        their wealth—
and they wanted an
        absolute,
        unequivocal,
        unqualified answer from the Baptizer.

Trying hard to evade questions he had no answers to, the Baptizer continued baptizing people drawn to the river by hope and faith. But the unruly crowds persisted, their voices ringing, clamoring all the louder,
        "What kind of clothing does the Messiah
           wear?"
        "What color is his hair?"
        "Is he slim?"

The Baptizer replied, "I don't know." They persisted still further,
        "What road does he travel?"
        "Is he with anyone?"

Finally John
        stopped baptizing,
        stepped forward,
        met the crowds face-to-face
        and calmly as ever spoke,
"The Messiah, the one who is to come, is in each of you,

if you allow your hearts
    enough space
    enough room,
if you allow yourselves *freedom*,
if you allow peace to guide your expectations."

Today, as we listen to the Baptizer,
    let us not look for the Messiah in a crib;
    let us look for the risen Lord
        in our own selves,
        in our own hearts.
And if we cannot find him there, let us not continue to be
blind but let us
    transform ourselves,
    reform ourselves,
for that joy of finding him will be overwhelming and that
is what keeps that child's birth a treasured event year
after year!

■ "And who is my neighbor?"
(The Good Samaritan Parable)

15th Sunday of Ordinary Time (C)   **Luke 10:25-37**

In any given society, laws are mandatory. One cannot
have a society without these instruments of order.

In our country, the laws are established for our good and
well-being. Without controlling or enslaving us, laws give
us the structure we as a society need. Each of us, however,
is affected by these laws every moment of our lives. Laws
give us protection and guarantee us the "rights" we are
endowed with. Laws are never meant to be an intrusion to
our basic freedom—yet, we know the consequences when
laws are broken. For example:

> We know what to expect when running
>   a red light and looking at our rear-view
>   mirror to see flashing red and blue lights.
> We know what's going to happen to us
>   if we pop our neighbor on the head: *a suit*!
> We know when running short of cash,
>   robbing a bank is no solution—unless you

like striped clothing and being even further
in debt!

Laws can be a benefit to us even though they are
restrictive. For example:
>We know that being hooked on drugs is
>against the law.
>We also know they hurt mind and body.
>We know that restaurants
>and supermarkets are constantly
>and stringently regulated, for the food they
>sell is the food that we eat!

The law during Jesus' lifetime was far from what we
understand as law. The Law of Jesus' time referred to
Jewish religious law and its interpretation and it stymied
the very freedom for which humans were created.

The Law that Jesus was referring to in our scripture
reading of the Good Samaritan parable was blindly
observed by the Jewish people. The common people as
well as the elite were obliged to follow the tenets of their
religion. And those included the Scribes, the Pharisees,
the Levites, the lawyers and the priests. All were subject
to the "letter of the Law." It was that kind of obedience to
"the letter of the Law" that offended Jesus.

Following the law was fine with Jesus, but he frowned
when the authoritarian institution made his Father's
people slaves to the Law. Jesus strenuously objected to
this form of control because it demeaned the very core and
heart of humanity. Jesus felt the purpose of his Father's
creation was for people to care for one another. Jewish
institutions like the Temple and the Synagogues taught
that one's observance of the Law was the highest praise
one could offer to God.

What disturbed Jesus most of all was the fact that the Law was too confining and impersonal; too structured and legalistic—the complete opposite of his Father's intention for the human beings his Father created.

So that when questioned about "What must I do to inherit eternal life?" and "Who is my neighbor?" Jesus replied with a story, a parable that has withstood the test of time.

Jesus told a story about a Jewish man who lay bleeding on the side of the road.

Two experts in the tradition of Jewish law saw the man and kept going about their business. Incidentally, these two religious men were on their way to offer sacrifice to Yahweh and the reason they did not stop is because the Law prohibited defilement (the touching of blood) prior to the offering to God. Though the two experts probably cared about this man who was near death, Jesus used an "outcast," a Samaritan, to show the questioner the real meaning of caring, and what his Father truly desired as an offering.

Jesus did nothing to shame the two religious—his intention was to shame the Law. Jesus knew these two men were following what they sincerely believed to be what his Father wanted. It simply never occurred to them that the personal Law of Love took precedence.

The reason this parable has never become outdated is because each of us has experienced events similar.

In my case, as I was leaving a graduation service a few years ago, I made an appointment with a priest-friend to have a pizza and beer together. We decided to meet at a favorite place since we had separate cars and my friend had an errand to run first. When pulling out of the church driveway onto the main highway in a teeming rain storm and dense fog, the likes of which I had never seen before, my car was hit broadside by a truck. The impact of the accident left my car and me in a ditch on the side of the road. Though I was unhurt, my pride was certainly heavily damaged. In the midst of all the fog and rain, the trucker and myself began to do those kinds of things one does when involved in an accident.

It so happened that a car stopped with two priests in it. They were at the same graduation ceremony as I had been just minutes before. I was really pleased to see them because at times like this, it is always good to have people there who care for you and that you can depend on. However, what transpired was not what I expected. The priest on the passenger side lowered his window just slightly to ask if I was okay. I guess I understood why he lowered his window only slightly since it was I who was out in the rain. My knee-jerk reaction to his question was a normal "I'm okay," but all he had to do was to take a serious look at me to conclude that I really needed help. The two priests accepted my answer as definitive and told me to "take care" of myself and left to go elsewhere—perhaps, to get a pizza and beer together! You can imagine what I said under my breath, "You *&$@%!"

It was just then that an elderly lady came up to me in the midst of the storm and told me that she knew me though I probably wouldn't know her and offered to assist me in any way possible. Being somewhat embarrassed at the sight of this lady in all the rain, I told her that I was fine and that everything was going to be okay. Though I was appreciative, I urged the lady to go home before she caught her death of cold. She wavered a bit but said that if that was best for me she would. Off she went as the police car arrived.

After about twenty minutes in the police car exchanging information with the other driver, the officer asked us if we knew "the elderly lady" who pulled up in her car behind us. Exclaiming that I knew this person, I approached her car with unbelieving eyes, and asked, "What are you doing here?" The lady, though apologetic, said she wasn't going to take "no" for an answer. She intended to wait for me so that she could make sure that I would be okay. She was going to follow me home—*and she did!*

The lady in this story broke all the conventional rules of safety: alone, in the rain, in the dark of night, at her age and with all her fears, to assist someone she truly barely knew. That was the Good Samaritan!

When I got home that night I searched inside me for all the anger that I felt for the two priests who left me standing on the side of the road in all that wet and nasty weather. I continued to blast them under my breath. Then it dawned on me that Jesus wasn't telling that parable to admonish the two religious men but to say that they were so controlled by the Law that simple compassion was never an option to their thinking. It took an "outcast" to show how compassion applies to our daily entanglements.

It also dawned on me that night that this parable could apply to me. Have I ever left someone dangling when help was critical or did I abide by the Law of a given moment? How about in the future? Will the Law or my neighbor control my compassion?

■ Scripture Index

Other Collections by Lou Ruoff

NO KIDDING, GOD, WHERE ARE YOU?
Parables of Ordinary Experience

Lou Ruoff

Paper, 106 pages, 5½" x 8½", ISBN 0-89390-141-5

The author shows you where he finds God: in a bottle of whiteout, in a hand of poker, in a game of hopscotch. These twenty-five stories work effectively as homilies and as ways to find God in everyday life. To help you with your planning, they are accompanied by Scripture references according to the season of the liturgical year.

PARABLES OF BELONGING:
Discipleship and Commitment in Everyday Life

Lou Ruoff

Paper, 112 pages, 5½" x 8½", ISBN 0-89390-253-5

The collection of stories in *Parables of Belonging* recognizes the ability of average people to minister to others in their lives just by carrying out their day-to-day activities. Telling these stories will help listeners acknowledge and rejoice in their own hidden giftedness and invigorate your community.

FOR GIVE: Stories of Reconciliation

Lou Ruoff

Paper, 120 pages, 5½" x 8½", ISBN 0-89390-198-9

In this collection of original stories, Lou Ruoff focuses on gospel reconciliation stories: "The Prodigal Son," "The Unforgiving Servant," "Seventy-Times-Seven," and more. Great for homily ideas, for catechesis, or for Re-membering Church sessions.

Call Toll-Free 1-888-273-7782 for current prices.
See last page for ordering information.

Storytelling Resources

STORYTELLING STEP BY STEP

Marsh Cassady, Ph.D.

Paper, 156 pages, 5½" x 8½", ISBN 0-89390-183-0

Marsh Cassady, a director, actor, and storyteller, shows you all the steps to successful storytelling: selecting the right story for your audience, adapting your story for different occasions, analyzing it so that you can present it well, preparing your audience, and presenting the story. Includes many examples of stories.

STORY AS A WAY TO GOD: A Guide for Storytellers

H. Maxwell Butcher

Paper, 153 pages, 5½" x 8½", ISBN 0-89390-201-2

Why are stories so powerful? This book reveals the dynamics of good storytelling. Find out why every good story from "The Ugly American" to "West Side Story" says something about the divine. Learn how to find God's story everywhere and how to tell it.

Resources for Preaching & Teaching

STORY POWER!
Compelling Illustrations for Preaching and Teaching
James A. Feehan

Paper, 120 pages, 5½" x 8½", ISBN 0-89390-304-3

To really get your point across you've got to tell stories. Good ones. Short ones. Powerful ones. Stories that intrigue. Stories that fascinate. Stories that capture the imagination. And then—since you're not just in the entertainment business—your stories have to hook your listeners to the gospel message. A tall order. This book by famed Irish preacher James Feehan will help. It's packed with dozens of anecdotes, quick story illustrations, and great tips for more powerful storytelling. A must for preachers and teachers.

SEASONAL ILLUSTRATIONS FOR PREACHING AND TEACHING
Donald L. Deffner

Paper, 176 pages, 5½" x 8½", ISBN 0-89390-234-9

Preachers and teachers: use these 175 illustrations to get your listeners' attention and enrich their understanding of the church year. These short bits will always make them think.

SERMONS FOR SERMON HATERS
Andre Papineau

Paper, 144 pages, 5½" x 8½", ISBN 0-89390-229-2

It's a preacher's dream—to turn on the turned-off. Thirty-four model sermons that show you how to break open the Gospel in ways that reach even the most jaded.

Call Toll-Free 1-888-273-7782 for current prices.
See last page for ordering information.

Resources for Preaching & Teaching

THE DREAM CATCHER:
Lectionary-Based Stories for Teaching and Preaching
James L. Henderschedt

Paper, 128 pages, 5½" x 8½", ISBN 0-89390-339-6

"Clever, poignant, humorous, in touch with our human reality, his stories, once read, are not the end, but rather the beginning of insight into my journey toward a loving God..." — Father Edward Miller, pastor, St. Bernardine's Catholic Church

HOMILY RESOURCES: From Celebrating The Lectionary
Edited by Liz Montes

Looseleaf, 312 pages, 8½" x 11", ISBN 0-89390-384-1

Published annually in August.

Helpful reflections on the Sunday readings that help you think without telling you what to think. Use independently or coordinate with the CTL curriculum. Covers every Sunday of the year from the first Sunday in September through the last Sunday in August each year.

WINDOWS INTO THE LECTIONARY:
Seasonal Anecdotes for Preaching and Teaching
Donald L. Deffner

Paper, 160 pages, 5½" x 8½", ISBN 0-89390-393-0

Preachers love a good anecdote, an evocative story, or a short illustration. Too often, they can only find items that fall flat because they a) don't fit the reading, b) don't connect to real life, c) make simplistic analogies, or d) don't have a punchline. No such problem with this collection. Homiletics professor Donald Deffner has made a significant effort to locate short sermon illustrations that work on all levels. This collection packs a punch. The illustrations carry a universal spiritual truth that can be applied to the hearer's personal world. Many stories have a telling climax. All of them are connected to the church year — and there is an index that enables you to search for stories by season, theme, or scripture verse.

Call Toll-Free 1-888-273-7782 for current prices.
See last page for ordering information.

Resources for Healing Ministry

BREAKTHROUGH: Stories of Conversion

Andre Papineau

Paper, 139 pages, 5½" x 8½", ISBN 0-89390-128-8

Witness what takes place inside Papineau's characters as they change, and the stories will remind you that change, ultimately, is a positive experience. Reflections following each section will help you help others deal with their personal conversions.

BIBLICAL BLUES: Growing Through Setups and Letdowns

Andre Papineau

Paper, 226 pages, 5½" x 8½", ISBN 0-89390-157-1

This book of biblical stories will take you deep into your own personal recovery and transform you. The author, whose dramatic tales always have a psychological edge, addresses how people set themselves up for letdowns. Great for personal reflection and some group discussions.

JESUS ON THE MEND: Healing Stories for Ordinary People

Andre Papineau

Paper, 150 pages, 5½" x 8½", ISBN 0-89390-140-7

Eighteen imaginative stories based on the Gospels illustrate four aspects of healing our brokenness: "Acknowledging the Need", "Reaching Out for Help", "The Healer's Credentials", and "The Healer's Therapy". Following each story is a reflection on the process of healing that takes place. Indexed to the lectionary.

Order from your local bookseller, or contact:

Resource Publications, Inc.
160 E. Virginia Street #290
San Jose, CA 95112-5876
1-408-286-8505
1-408-287-8748 (fax)
Order Toll-Free:
1-888-273-7782

NE